New to the Parish

Stories of Love, War and Adventure
from Ireland's Immigrants

Sorcha Pollak

NEW ISLAND

NEW TO THE PARISH
First published in 2018 by
New Island Books
16 Priory Hall Office Park
Stillorgan
County Dublin
Republic of Ireland

www.newisland.ie

Print ISBN: 978-1-84840-678-0
Epub ISBN: 978-1-84840-679-7
Mobi ISBN: 978-1-84840-680-3

British Library Cataloguing Data.

A CIP catalogue record for this book is available from the British Library.

Typeset by JVR Creative India
Cover design by Kate Gaughran
Printed by TJ International Ltd, Padstow, Cornwall

New Island Books is a member of Publishing Ireland.

Contents

For my parents, Andy and Doireann.

Glossary of Terms

Migrant: A migrant is someone who moves from one place to another in order to live in another country. According to the International Organisation for Migration, over one billion people in the world are migrants, or more than one in seven people globally.

Asylum seeker: An asylum seeker is a person who has left their country of origin because of a fear of persecution for reasons of race, religion, nationality, membership of a particular social group or political opinion. An asylum seeker formally applies to the host state for a declaration as a refugee, and is legally entitled to remain in that state until their application is decided. They must demonstrate their fear of persecution is well founded and must remain an asylum seeker until their application for refugee status is processed (the Irish government believes that some asylum seekers are in fact economic migrants). An asylum seeker becomes a refugee if their application for protection as a refugee is successful. In 2016 there were 2.8 million asylum seekers globally.

Refugee: A refugee is someone who has been forced to flee his or her country because of persecution, war or violence. A refugee has a well-founded fear of persecution for reasons of race, religion, nationality, political opinion or membership of a particular social group. Most likely, they cannot return home or are afraid to do so. Refugees are protected under the 1951 UN Refugee Convention, which Ireland has signed and ratified. More than half the world's refugees come from just three countries: Syria, Afghanistan and South Sudan. Another 5.2 million refugees come from Palestine.

Programme refugees: A programme refugee is a person who is given leave to enter and remain in the State for temporary protection or who has been resettled as part of a group in response to a humanitarian crisis and at the request of the UN High Commissioner for Refugees. Since 2000, more than 1,800 refugees from almost thirty countries, including Iraq and Syria, have been admitted as programme refugees for resettlement in Ireland.

Irish Refugee Protection Programme: The Irish Refugee Protection Programme was established in September 2015 as a response to the migration crisis in southern Europe. Under the programme, the Irish government pledged to accept up to 4000 people into the State within two years—2,622 people through EU relocation from Italy and Greece and 1,040 programme refugees through resettlement from camps in Lebanon and Jordan. By December 2017, 1,502 people had arrived in Ireland.

Internally displaced person: These are people who are forced to flee their homes but do not cross international borders.

Some 40.3 million people worldwide are internally displaced, according to the UNHCR.

Economic migrant: An economic migrant is a person who has left his or her country to find employment in another country. Citizens of all EU countries have the right to come to Ireland to seek employment.

EEA national: A national of the European Economic Area, which is made up of all EU member states along with Iceland, Liechtenstein and Norway. The latter three countries are members of the EU's single market but not of the European Union itself. Switzerland is neither an EU nor an EEA member but is part of the single market, meaning Swiss people have the same rights to live and work in other European countries as other EEA nationals.

Non-Irish national: A person who is not a citizen of Ireland.

Direct provision: The Irish system for accommodating asylum seekers. Established in 2000, the system was set up to provide shelter to asylum seekers for six months whilst their application for refugee status is being processed. The vast majority of asylum seekers spend much longer than six months in the system and in 2016 the average length of stay was nearly three years. They are accommodated in privately run centres which provide food and board for residents. Asylum seekers in Ireland are not allowed to work (although this may change for some of them following a May 2017 ruling of the Supreme Court) and are not entitled to the usual social welfare payments. As of

June 2017, asylum seeking adults receive a weekly cash allowance of €21.60. The allowance for children was also raised to €21.60 per week.

Introduction

Stephen Pollak knew very little about Ireland the day he stepped off a plane in Belfast airport seventy years ago. Like the small number who had come before him and the many hundreds of thousands that would follow, he had arrived on this small island on the fringes of Western Europe to begin a new life. After more than a decade of war, journalism, clandestine work and imprisonment, life in rural Ireland would have felt very foreign to this Czech immigrant. The hospitality he received from a Northern Irish family that was totally disconnected from his previously dangerous and fractured life—as a left-wing Jew in wartime Europe—serves as a reminder of how important a warm welcome can be.

Stephen Pollak was my grandfather. He arrived at my maternal great-grandparents house in Kellswater, outside Ballymena in County Antrim in April 1948 as a political refugee who had come to Ireland to join my grandmother, Eileen Gaston, after a whirlwind affair and subsequent marriage in Prague. She was pregnant with my father who was born a month later. Eileen had moved to Prague after the Second World War to teach English and there, in February 1947, at a party after an ice hockey match between

Czechoslovakia and the USA, she met a young journalist named Stephen.

Born in Berlin in 1913 to prosperous Jewish parents from Bohemia, Stephen renounced his privileged upbringing of boarding schools and skiing holidays and left art school in London to join the International Brigades and fight in the Spanish Civil War. He was badly wounded—walking with a heavy limp for the rest of his life—in the battle for Madrid in 1937 and became a Communist sympathiser in the years that followed. After he recovered from his injuries he worked as an undercover courier for the Communist Party, travelling around Central and Eastern Europe with a fake Canadian identity. In 1941 he was arrested by the British authorities in India for being a Communist spy and was imprisoned for the duration of World War II in the city of Dehra Dun in the foothills of the Himalayas.

He returned to Europe in 1946 and found work as a journalist with a left-wing English language magazine in Prague. However, after the Communists seized power in February 1948, and despite his Communist sympathies, my grandfather was accused of writing in support of US policies, lost his job and was visited by the secret police. He acted quickly and booked my heavily pregnant grandmother onto a flight back to Britain. Shortly afterwards he fled the country on foot, walking over the border into Austria under cover of darkness before flying to London en route to Northern Ireland. While my grandparents only remained in County Antrim for a short while after my father was born— they eventually moved to London—my grandmother's Presbyterian family welcomed this strange, limping young foreigner with great kindness. They and their neighbours in that small rural community were able to see through the brash exterior of this adventurous young man to the humanity which lay beneath—to a lonely exile who had lost family and friends during a decade of war and displacement, but who had finally found love and acceptance in the arms of a young Irish woman.

In recent years people have often asked why I express such interest in the lives of refugees. What is it about their plight and suffering that inspires me to tell their stories? Like nearly every Irish person, I am descended on my mother's side from emigrants (from Cork) who left for the United States. However, I am also the descendent of an immigrant—a person with nowhere else to go who came to this country as a refugee. I have grown up with the awareness that had my mother's Northern Irish family not welcomed my grandfather, the future of my own family could have turned out very differently.

Growing up in Ireland in the 1980s and 1990s my Polish surname was considered exotic. Ireland was a culturally homogenous island with very little understanding or experience of immigration. And why would we? Several centuries of hunger, poverty and unemployment hardly made this small island an attractive destination. However, there were some, like my grandfather, who did arrive on Irish shores in the late nineteenth and early-mid twentieth century. They were not always made welcome: we pride ourselves on being the home of one hundred thousand welcomes, yet ours has not always been a very noble history when it comes to those in need.

In the late nineteenth and early twentieth century a small number of Jewish people arrived in Ireland, many of them seeking asylum from increasing anti-Semitism in Russia. There were an estimated 4,800 Jews in Ireland by 1904, most of them in Dublin but some also in Cork and Limerick. Their welcome in that latter city was short-lived and in early 1904, 35 families living there were attacked and forced to leave in what became known as the Limerick 'pogrom'. The Irish response to German and Austrian Jewish refugees fleeing the Nazi regime in the 1930s and 1940s, was unwelcoming, with the government implementing an extremely restrictive refugee policy. In the mid 1940s the Department of Justice initially refused to allow 100 Jewish orphaned children, survivors of Bergen-Belsen concentration camp, a temporary refuge in Ireland, calling Jews 'a potential irritant in the body politic.' Taoiseach Éamon De Valera eventually allowed the children into Ireland on a temporary basis.

In 1956 Ireland welcomed 540 refugees from Hungary following the Soviet invasion. However the new arrivals quickly became disillusioned with being housed in army barracks in County Clare and went on hunger strike to draw attention to their 'sit and rust' existence. The immigrants—many of whom had worked as miners, technicians and craftsmen in Hungary—argued that while Ireland had accepted them as refugees, the State did not care about their future. The vast majority of them eventually left Ireland and moved to the United States and Canada.

In 1973 voluntary and charity groups lobbied for the Irish government to offer refuge to Chilean refugees fleeing from General Pinochet's right-wing military coup. However the Department of Justice argued that Irish society was 'less cosmopolitan than that of Western European countries generally and in consequence, the absorption of even a limited number of foreigners would prove extremely difficult'. It also expressed fear at the political ideologies of these Chilean arrivals, saying that most of them had become refugees because 'they are Marxist and probably communists'. The government eventually agreed to admit around 120 Chilean refugees. In the years that followed groups of Vietnamese, Iranian, Bosnian, Kosovar, Kurdish, Sudanese, Congolese and Burmese (Rohingya and Karen ethnic minorities) asylum seekers, as well as people from other countries, would also be resettled in Ireland.

While Ireland did become one of the first six countries in Europe to establish a UN-sponsored resettlement programme in 1998 for refugees fleeing war and persecution, our nation's claim of being able to empathise with migrant suffering given our own turbulent past does not always ring true. Our current record of providing refuge to asylum seekers fleeing conflict and poverty in the Middle East, Africa and South Asia remains underwhelming. In October 2017 there were 4,838 women, men and children living in direct provision—a system established in 2000 as a temporary housing solution for asylum seekers. In 2016 residents were spending an average of nearly three years waiting for a decision on their status (i.e. whether and on what basis they are going to be allowed to stay in Ireland). While the question of asylum seekers' right to work was finally addressed in May 2017, when the Supreme Court ruled that it was unconstitutional to prevent people in direct provision from seeking work, many question marks remain over the length of time people spend in these centres and the conditions they live in. Meanwhile the Irish Government's target of welcoming 4,000 asylum seekers from camps in Greece, Italy, Lebanon and Jordan is minute when compared to the hundreds of thousands of people accepted by countries like Germany and Sweden since 2015.

Nearly three years ago I began writing a series for *The Irish Times* about people who had come to live in Ireland. While *New to the Parish* did coincide with a barrage of reports about asylum seekers moving en masse towards Europe, the series did not happen because of the migrant crisis. The idea stemmed from the increasing diversity in Irish society that has developed over the past ten to twenty years. The hope was to offer an insight into the motivations of the immigrant, be they a student seeking education, a skilled worker looking for new opportunities or a mother and child fleeing civil war. In this book I hope to provide a deeper understanding of what makes a person leave their native land, often in extreme difficulty, in order to start a new life abroad. Each of these fourteen stories are completely different; some came to Ireland for work; others for education; some retired here; others fell in love with an Irish person. Some came here out of necessity, forced from their homes by death and destruction. But they all have one thing in common: they are all migrants.

Interspersed between these personal stories—which run chronologically from the enlargement of the European Union in 2004 to the inauguration of Donald Trump in 2017—I offer the reader a brief snapshot, year by year, of the context behind them: the mass migration of people across national boundaries in search of a better life, which is one of the defining issues of our globalised age. This is not an in-depth or academic study. It is one Irish journalist's view, based on interviews with individual actors in this great drama; the drama of what Ivan Krastev, the Bulgarian political scientist, has called the 'revolution' of the twenty-first century.

Migration is not a new phenomenon—we humans are migratory creatures. But in this technologically advanced era, the migrant crisis of recent years has been broadcast to a worldwide audience. People can no longer turn a blind eye to the crises unfolding on the borders of Greece or Lebanon, Mexico or Bangladesh. Awareness is just a click away through Twitter, Facebook and Instagram. However, understanding and empathy require greater effort. These stories are my small contribution to enhancing this empathy so that, like my great-grandparents in County Antrim all those years ago, our nation has the confidence and compassion to open our doors and truly live up to our reputation as the home of *céad míle fáilte.*

2004 Migration

On Saturday 1 May 2004, Irish Nobel Laureate Seamus Heaney stood on the steps of Farmleigh House in Dublin's Phoenix Park and read his poem 'Beacons at Bealtaine'. Written specially for the European Union enlargement celebrations, Heaney's poetry captured the palpable sense of achievement and possibility that filled the air that bright sunny Saturday as leaders from twenty-five member states gathered in Dublin to celebrate the expansion of the EU project. On that day, the European Union, which had begun as just six countries—Belgium, France, Germany, Italy, Luxembourg and the Netherlands—spread east to incorporate ten new nations into its political and economic alliance. Cyprus, the Czech Republic, Estonia, Hungary, Latvia, Lithuania, Malta, Poland, Slovakia and Slovenia were welcomed into a project which began in 1950 with the goal of ending centuries of war and bloodshed in Europe.

The Union, which had grown from 6 to 15 member states over the latter half of the twentieth century—including the accession of Ireland with Denmark and the United Kingdom in January 1973—sought to achieve a society where inclusion, tolerance, justice, solidarity and non-discrimination would prevail. An *Irish Times* editorial published on 1 May noted that enlargement was

> 'the greatest achievement of the EU's foreign pol-
> icy, bringing peaceful transformation to most of
> Europe at a time when the Balkan wars pointed up
> the danger of different outcomes. For most of the
> new EU member-states, today's events represent
> a final liberation from that Soviet and commu-
> nist tyranny—even though they have exchanged
> incorporation in one form of international union
> for another. The central difference is that the EU
> is a voluntary union of states whose equality is
> legally recognised.'[1]

It is clear that 2004 was a time of great positivity and optimism for the European Union. Nearly a decade had passed
since the Balkans conflict and the barrier that once divided
the continent between communist east and capitalist west was
becoming a distant memory. While the 2003 Iraq war had
arguably triggered a divide across Europe between those who
supported or rejected armed intervention in that conflict, the
freedom, democracy and protection of human rights promised
by the Union seemed increasingly achievable.

The Irish State, which held the EU presidency at the time of
enlargement and was in the middle of an economic boom, was
eager to invite central and eastern European job seekers into the
country to help with the rapid expansion and growth of twenty-
first century Ireland. The many workers who began arriving on
Irish shores during the summer of 2004 from Poland, Latvia,

Lithuania and other central and eastern European countries were for the most part welcomed with open arms into the construction, hospitality, agriculture and retail industries.

John O'Brennan, a lecturer in European politics at the National University of Ireland Maynooth, later wrote that between 2002 and 2012, 'the UK and Ireland proved amongst the most favoured destinations for new member state nationals, not just because of the attractive employment prospects they offered, but because English is now unquestionably the dominant language in a world of technologically driven globalisation'.[2]

The results of the 2002 Irish census showed that the Polish presence in the Republic was nearly non-existent with just 2,124 Poles recorded in April of that year. The census, carried out just over two years before EU enlargement, also showed there were just 2,104 Lithuanians and 1,797 Latvians living in Ireland. By 2006 the number of Poles had skyrocketed to 63,276, while the number of Lithuanians had risen to 24,468 and Latvians to 13,319.

In 2002 the number of immigrants from countries outside Europe was slightly higher than arrivals from eastern European nations, but still relatively low when compared with later statistics. The census of that year found 8,969 Nigerians, 5,842 Chinese, and 4,185 South Africans living in Ireland. By 2006 there were 16,300 Nigerians and 11,161 Chinese people in Ireland, with just a small rise to 5,432 for South Africans.

While the initial response to this rise in immigration was positive among many Irish people, a fear of different races, cultures and beliefs did begin to gradually spread among some communities. This distrust was bolstered by rumours that many of the women arriving from African countries were pregnant and came with the sole aim of ensuring Irish citizenship for their newborn child. The response from the Irish Government, or more specifically Minister for Justice Michael McDowell, was to hold a referendum to change the rules around the constitutional entitlement to citizenship by birth.

McDowell described people coming into Ireland to give birth to children and secure Irish citizenship as 'citizenship tourists', but rejected claims that the vote was racist. Taoiseach Bertie Ahern also rejected suggestions that the referendum would undermine the human rights of children born in Ireland. The Labour Party, which opposed the change to the constitution, warned the referendum would 'encourage racist tendencies'. Michael D Higgins, who was Labour party president at the time, described McDowell's proposal as 'shameful and disgraceful' and said he could not accept a change that would mean two children born in the same maternity ward on the same day would enjoy different legal and constitutional rights.

The referendum was held on 11 June 2004 and passed with an overwhelming 79.17% voting against giving Irish citizenship to every child born in Ireland. Under the new legislation, Irish citizenship could only be granted to children with at least one parent who was an Irish citizen, or entitled to Irish citizenship, at the time of their birth. Before 1999 the right to citizenship by reason of birth in Ireland had existed in ordinary law. Automatic entitlement to Irish citizenship at birth had been in place since a constitutional amendment in 1999 which stated: 'It is the entitlement and birthright of every person born in the island of Ireland, which includes its islands and seas, to be part of the Irish nation.' This birthright ceased to exist on 1 January 2005.

Dr Aoileann Ní Mhurchú, lecturer in international politics at the University of Manchester, later wrote that automatic citizenship at birth was almost universally associated as 'a more inclusive way of regulating citizenship than that of citizenship by descent'. Ní Mhurchú argued that birthright citizenship was necessary for integration and to 'ensure that illegality is not passed down through generations of migrants'.[3]

As the Irish citizenship debate continued throughout 2004, international fears of terrorist activity in Europe began gaining momentum after a series of bombings in Madrid. On 11 March 2004, 192 people died and more than 2,000 were injured when ten bombs packed with nails and dynamite exploded on four trains heading into central Madrid. It later emerged that the bombings had been carried out by a group of young men, mostly from north Africa, who according to prosecutors were inspired by an Al-Qaeda affiliated website that called for attacks on Spain.

The previous year the Spanish conservative government had strongly backed the American invasion in Iraq despite polls that showed more than 90% of Spaniards were opposed to intervention. It was felt by many that the 2004 Madrid bombings were a response from Islamic militants to Spanish involvement in the Iraqi conflict and a warning message to the rest of Europe that it too could fall victim to terrorist activity if it embraced the American war effort.

Despite the growing antagonism and divergent opinions among European member states over whether or not involvement in the Iraq war could trigger future terrorist attacks, EU leaders still pushed ahead with the enlargement celebrations in Dublin that May. Highlighting the achievements of the Union, Taoiseach Bertie Ahern called on attendees to remember that 'from war we have created peace, from hatred we have created respect, from division we have created union, from dictatorship and oppression we have created vibrant and sturdy democracies; from poverty we have created prosperity.'[4]

Bassam Al-Sabah, 2004

Whenever Bassam Al-Sabah mentions in conversation that he spent the first decade of his life in Iraq, he nearly always detects a note of pity in people's response. 'I feel like they don't know how to react to that information. I think people are interested but they also don't want to get too political. It's like someone who hasn't come from that background feels they should respond in a certain way. But for a person who is actually from Iraq, you just lived there. There's no pity about that for us. It was our life.'

In fact, when people ask where he comes from, Bassam prefers to say Balbriggan rather than Ireland or Iraq. 'It depends on how the person asks the question but it's often very like "oh, I see you're not from here, where are you actually from?" I say Balbriggan because I like seeing the confusion on their faces. It's this moment of "wait, but you don't look Irish. What?" Sometimes I forget I look different and that question is a reminder that for many Irish people you are different. Most of the time it's not out of malice that people ask these questions, they're just interested. But at a certain point I do just say I'm from Iraq, it's easier.'

Rather than talk about his Iraqi heritage, Bassam prefers using his artistic talents to reflect on the childhood he spent in a country that since the mid-2000s has become synonymous with war and violence. In 2016, following his graduation from the Dún Laoghaire Institute of Art, Design and Technology (IADT), the young artist was selected as one of the thirteen best graduating artists in Ireland and awarded a place to exhibit at the RDS visual art awards. He was also the recipient of the Royal Hibernian Academy 2016 graduate award which gave him the use of a studio at the RHA in Dublin for a year.

The idea behind the twenty-three-year-old's latest exhibition stems from the media coverage of the Iraq war and the lens through which he believes the western world perceives life for Iraqi citizens. 'Every time the news reported that a bomb had gone off we had real context because my grandmother would get on the phone and call someone to get the actual story. How big was it? Was everyone OK? Where was it? She doesn't trust the news anymore because they're always trying to sell the event as a story. It's fair that the media have to get people to watch the news but they also have to do the story justice and explain what really happened rather than sensationalising everything.'

His art also examines the role cartoons play in 'the distortion between fantasy and reality', particularly for children growing up in a conflict zone. 'When I was a child I didn't understand that war was a violent thing because I equated it to what we saw in cartoons. All the cartoons were based around a hero and in the context of Iraq that hero was part of the army. That's how fantasy can slip into reality without you noticing. You hear a bomb going off but you equate it to what you see in a cartoon so it never feels like something violent. That's something I'm really interested in, what cartoons actually meant to kids as they grow up.' As a child, Bassam found it difficult to make sense of the violence unfolding around him. 'When you're ten years old you don't really know what's going on and your parents aren't going to take the time to explain because you're so lost anyway. The only time I really understood was when a bomb went off close to a family member's home and everyone was calling to make sure they were OK. But whenever people ask me about my experience in Iraq I like to point out that we had an extremely sheltered childhood and kind of grew up in a bubble'.

His work is deeply influenced by the sense of displacement that comes with being shifted from one culture to another. In 2004, shortly before his tenth birthday, Bassam, his mother, his grandmother and his sister left their home in Iraq to join their father in Ireland. His father, an engineer, left Iraq when Bassam was six years old after he found a job in Dublin. He began applying for visas to bring his wife, children and mother to join him in Europe but failed to secure the documentation before the outbreak of the Iraq war. 'When my dad moved here he rented a room with an Irish couple who were very kind and taught him all about Ireland. They gave him Irish history books and books with folklore and fairy tales so he could really absorb the culture of the place. They eased him into life in Ireland and then he was able to do the same for us. We were supposed to move out here before the war but the visa process was very slow, it took years.'

When Bassam's father told his employers he needed to return home to see his family after the US invasion in 2003, the organisation's response was that he would have a job in Ireland whenever he returned. Back in Iraq, his family was slowly growing accustomed to living in a country no longer under the control of Saddam Hussein. Shortly after the American invasion, a stream of western music and films began flowing into Iraq, which for so long had been cut off from western media by strict censorship rules. 'Before the war, Iraq was very censored and controlled. Western music was banned and if there was a movie shown in Iraq it would be a completely different version of what you would see here because it would be censored and dubbed in a certain way. After the invasion we had this influx of media coming into the country. We experienced the 1990s and 2000s all at once. We got Christina Aguilera in her Disney phase, her "Genie in a Bottle" phase and her "Dirty" phase all at once. Westlife, Boyzone and the Backstreet Boys all happened at the same time. It was all bootleg CDs so you'd buy a Celine Dion CD and it was Britney Spears inside.'

Bassam and his older sister were fascinated by the stories of their father's life in Ireland and showed a particular interest in the Argos catalogue he brought back on his visit home. 'We had never seen that much stuff in one place. We'd look through it for days going "I'm gonna buy this, I'm gonna buy that". 'Living in a city of more than seven million people, it was almost impossible for Bassam and his family to imagine the world of a small, rainy island in Western Europe. When his father announced that the family would be following him back to Ireland, Bassam pored over a map of the world with his grandmother who squinted through her glasses to try and find the tiny Irish dot on the edge of the Atlantic.

In the summer of 2004 the family travelled to Syria to organise visas with the Irish consulate before flying to Ireland where they moved into their new home in Balbriggan. 'I think my memory is very linked to photos from the time but it's all kind of a daze. We went to Syria for a month because the border between Iraq and Syria was open at the time and there was no Irish embassy in Baghdad. We visited the embassy and they told us the visas would come through in a few weeks but then suddenly they arrived and we were told there was a flight that night. It was literally like boom, and then we were here.'

The family arrived in Dublin mid-summer which gave Bassam's father a chance to introduce his children to their new home before the school term kicked off. He began by showing them the shopping centre in Balbriggan and then introduced them to a larger shopping mall in Swords. Finally he brought them into the city centre where they visited museums and sites around Dublin. 'He made us go through a few steps before we could see the whole city. Back in Iraq I don't remember there being any shopping centres. There were a lot of markets and small kiosks for clothes but there wasn't a city centre with huge stores.'

Unlike his sister and mother who had learned basic English in Iraq, Bassam didn't speak a word of the language when he arrived in his new home. In September 2004 he began fourth class at the local Balbriggan primary school where his parents hoped he would pick up the language in the classroom. 'I had already finished fourth class in Iraq but repeated it in Ireland so it gave me a year to learn English as my main priority. I found the subjects quite easy, especially maths because in Iraq maths is quite intense. I think it was easy for me to learn English because I was young and put into a situation where you can't not speak the language,' says Bassam in his now strong Dublin accent. 'At the time the class was learning spelling which helped and I had to speak English to make friends. I think learning a language through speaking is a lot easier than learning from a book. You have to absorb it.'

Speaking in English was more difficult for Bassam's older sister. 'She already spoke a little bit from books in Iraq but I think it was harder for her to break her accent. I don't think I have an accent when I speak but she still has a hint of one. My parents also have a very tangy accent. There's a curve to it when they speak English.' Bassam believes the move was more of a challenge for his sister who was 14 years old when the family came to Ireland. 'I think things were different for her because she was a teenager. Even now I still think she would find life a bit distant here. But I feel like I've completely assimilated into the culture, there's nothing that seems weird to me anymore. I can make all the "Mammy" jokes now. You eventually understand all the layers of Irish humour.'

After he finished his Leaving Cert, Bassam decided he wanted to study art at IADT. His sister was also artistic but when she suggested pursing a career in the field her parents were not happy. 'The compromise was that she did architecture. She's older than me by four years so by the time I came around they were like "we're not having this fight again, just do whatever you want but do it well". I think my sister fought a lot of the fights for me.' Bassam understands why it may have been difficult for his parents, who both studied engineering, to support their children's desire to become artists. 'They come from a time and place where you went to college to leave the country and get a job. To them, art was like, "what is this?" They still don't particularly understand it. I think it would have been the same if I'd wanted to be a journalist or a writer. A doctor goes to college and then can get a job. But as a writer there are so many trajectories you can take. They wanted their kids to succeed but all they knew was this extreme, intense education and art was new to them. But then I was nominated for the RDS visual arts award and I got the RHA studio so that kind of quantified the skills for them. It's a success they can understand.'

Had the family remained in Iraq, Bassam realises he may have never had the opportunity to pursue his love of art. 'It's hard to know if I could have become an artist over there because I don't know what the education system is like or whether there's even an art college. We definitely wouldn't have had the money for me to study art abroad. I was always good at drawing so I think I might have become an architect or a designer. I don't think my work is necessarily ultra-political but it is politically charged. I would not have been able to do that in Iraq.'

One of the political topics which has played a role in Bassam's art is Ireland's debate about access to abortion. He became involved in the 'Repeal' movement in 2016 after his college lecturer invited him to join the Artists' Campaign to Repeal the Eighth Amendment. 'If you gather that many people together and say something loudly enough change will start to happen and people will learn from that. I think that's why the repeal movement is so great, because it feels like a community. Even if we don't all know each other, we're here for a very specific reason and fighting for the same thing. It's great to be able to do something like that because it feels right.' Bassam has discussed the abortion debate with his parents and grandmother and says they are all pro-choice. 'My parents are fairly liberal. They know what it was like to live in an Iraq where everything was controlled and they're deeply political because of the situation they grew up in.'

Bassam's father now works as a researcher in UCD and his mother works for Dún Laoghaire County Council. While they are happy in their work, Bassam believes his parents are still stuck in the 'survival mode' they developed during the Iraq war. 'They've been surviving for so long that they can't break out. They love their jobs so much that I worry they'll never retire. They only really settled here once they started making friends with Irish people. It helped them to finally feel a calmness because there wasn't this separation between I am this and you are that.' Life in Ireland has been slightly more difficult for his grandmother. 'I don't want to speak for her but I think it's quite sad because she hasn't had all her kids in the same place in twenty years. Everybody's all over the place. I have an aunt in California, an aunt in Dubai, an uncle in Oxford, there's part of the family in New Zealand, there's another aunt in Sweden. Now that they all have WhatsApp she's always on the phone to one of them.'

A few years ago Bassam's grandmother went back to Iraq to visit family and retrieve some of the items that were left behind in 2004. 'When we moved to Ireland we had fifty kilo suitcases with us, that was all we could take, so there was a lot of stuff left behind. My grandmother went back to the house but came back completely distraught saying "it wasn't like this when I left". She decided no one was touching what was left in the house and just burnt it all. In my mind I think she was actually happy to be burning everything because my dad and uncle were such hoarders. Finally the house was clean!'

The twenty-three-year-old artist, who has found a new studio space to use following his residency at the RHA, describes the Irish visual art world as small but supportive. 'Even if people don't like your work they'll go to your exhibition and say it was good. Ireland is a small country and therefore every community will be small within that. That can have its pros and cons. Because it's so small there will be a lot of favours. But on the other hand, it's small enough that you can ask for a favour.' While most of his work since college has focused on his experiences from Iraq, he's eager to develop new ideas for future projects. 'My experience of Iraq was nine years, five of which I don't remember because I was too young. So I only have four years to play with and I don't want to drag that out. You don't want to become that artist that constantly uses yourself as inspiration.'

In the summer of 2017, Bassam's older sister got married and four days later the couple moved to China. While his parents have struggled with their daughter's departure, they have always encouraged their children to travel and live abroad. 'They don't want to hold anyone back. I want to do an MA at some point and I would like to do it abroad. If I go, my parents will be sad but they'll also be happy. As much as they want us to stay here forever, they also want us to have our own life experiences.' Bassam is confident his sister and her husband will return to Ireland after a few years. 'She's twenty-seven and was like "I wanna get out of here, I'm gonna find myself." But she also said she couldn't leave forever because she knows what it's like to be separated from your family. She decided to go for a while and then she says she'll come back.'

While Bassam realises some people in Ireland will always view him as a foreigner, he feels a deep connection to the country he has called home for more than half his life. 'All my friends are here, my home is here. It's a deep feeling I have for Ireland. It's such a beautiful country, I love it here. Coming from Iraq this place was so calm and beautiful. I also love Ireland because it's still so untouched with so many trees and fields. I still love Iraq but I would never go back because I have such a bubble in my head of what it was like as a child and I don't want to burst that. Maybe the memory and the romantic idea of a place is better than the reality.'

2005 Migration

Historian Timothy Garton Ash wrote in the *New York Review of Books* in 2017 that:

> 'Had I been cryogenically frozen in January 2005 I would have gone to my provisional rest as a happy European … With the enlargement of the European Union to include many post-Communist democracies, the 1989 "return to Europe" dream of my Central European friends was coming true … Madrid, Warsaw, Athens, Lisbon and Dublin felt as if they were bathed in sunlight from windows newly opened in ancient dark places. The periphery of Europe was apparently converging with the continent's historic core around Germany, the Benelux countries, France and northern Italy. Young Spaniards, Greeks, Poles and Portuguese spoke optimistically about the new chances offered them by "Europe" … Even notoriously Euroskeptical Britain was embracing its European future under Prime Minister Tony Blair.'[5]

Garton Ash's idealised portrayal of Europe in 2005 seemed somewhat true at the time. Young Poles, Lithuanians and Latvians were arriving in the UK and Ireland in their hundreds of thousands, ready to work hard for a salary previously unimaginable in their eastern European homes. The United Kingdom held the presidency of the European Union for the latter six months of that year with Tony Blair declaring himself 'a passionate pro-European'. Speaking of his ambitions for the UK's presidency in June 2005, Blair called for member states to take stock of the many achievements of the EU and how it stood as 'a monument to political achievement.' 'Almost fifty years of peace, fifty years of prosperity, fifty years of progress,' said Mr Blair. 'Think of it and be grateful.'

However, underneath this veneer of optimism and hope for the future, many young Europeans—particularly young people from poor immigrant families—were beginning to fight back against an establishment they viewed as distant, elite and hostile to their needs. In Paris in October 2005, 4,700 people were arrested in the city's high unemployment 'banlieue' areas following riots caused by the deaths of two teenagers from African backgrounds who were trying to escape from police. The rioting went on for three weeks in marginalised suburbs across France. With ten thousand cars burned and three hundred buildings and schools torched, French interior minister Nicholas Sarkozy, the man en route to become the nation's next president, called for an end to riots by 'hooligans or scum'.

In the same month—Ceuta and Melilla, two Spanish enclaves on the North African coast—made headlines after six young men from West Africa were killed trying to climb the six-metre razor wire militarised fences separating the cities from the Moroccan territory surrounding them. Hundreds of young African men tried to scale the perilous fences each day in the hope of making it across to Europe. The European Commission warned of 'mounting migration pressure from Africa' which was 'likely to increase in the coming years.'[6] Having grown from 221 million inhabitants in 1950 to 800 million inhabitants in 2005, and without the requisite economic growth to match this surge in population, millions of Africans were living in poverty. Large-scale environmental degradation, such as drought, as well as violence in some regions had also played a role in forcing people from their homes. 'Misery and fear are pushing people out of their regions of origin in search of a better life in more stable and developed regions, first among them Europe,' wrote the Commission.[7]

The island of Lampedusa off the Italian coast also witnessed a surge in migrants with more than 10,000 arriving by boat during 2005. A total of 6,000 people had lost their lives trying to reach EU countries in the previous eleven years, most of them while crossing the Mediterranean from North Africa. This was to rise to more than 33,000 in the following twelve years.

Despite this rise in numbers crossing into Europe through Spain and Italy, the United Nations Refugee Agency reported a fall by half in the number of people applying for asylum in the world's industrialised countries in the five years leading up to 2005. The number of applications in the European Union fell to its lowest since 1988; applications in Denmark and Germany fell to their lowest number since 1983 and in the UK hit the lowest number since 1993. The UNHCR explained the drop in backlog as an indication that European asylum procedures had become more efficient. However, the Migrant Policy Institute attributed the decline to more restrictive asylum policies designed to discourage applicants. Greece was the only country to see a major increase in applications although most of this was accounted for by Georgians.

Ireland also experienced this drop in asylum seekers with applications for refugee status continuing to fall. There were 4,323 applications for asylum in Ireland, down from a peak of 11,634 in 2002. On the other hand, the Economic and Social Research Institute (ESRI) recorded a record high of 70,000 economic migrants—people who came both from inside and outside the EU looking for work—arriving in Ireland in 2005, mostly due to the large numbers of people arriving from EU accession states. The number of work permits issued fell substantially reflecting the fact that migrant workers from the new EU member states no longer needed a permit to work in Ireland. However, significant numbers of work permits continued to be issued to nationals from the Philippines, India, South Africa and North America.

While arrivals from eastern Europe were able to immediately apply for work and settle into their new Irish lifestyles, a total of 5,164 asylum seekers were stuck in direct provision centres waiting for an answer on their request for leave to the remain in the country. The direct provision system was established by the Government in 2000 as an 'interim solution' to the rising numbers of people seeking asylum in Ireland. The Reception and Integration Agency was created to oversee the new accommodation system and provide support to those applying for asylum. Before 2000, asylum seekers were able to access social welfare payments and rent supplements. Under the new system, asylum seekers received a weekly cash allowance of €19.10 per adult and €9.60 per child, and were prohibited from seeking work (a ban unique in the EU outside Lithuania). Even though the system was designed as short-term accommodation solution for people seeking asylum, it became increasingly clear throughout 2005 that residents were spending far longer than the originally projected six months in these hostels.

In March 2005, *Irish Times* journalist Kathy Sheridan wrote that thirty-five Nigerians had been repatriated from Dublin to Lagos for 'immigration related offences' in one day. In an article entitled 'How could I bring my children back to a place where they would not be safe?', Sheridan told the story of a woman named Nkechi Okolie and her three children who were deported to Nigeria after three years living in Castleblayney in County Monaghan. Okolie did not want to return to Nigeria for fear that her daughters would have to undergo female genital mutilation. Nevertheless, the family were put on a plane by gardaí and flown back to Nigeria where they were met in Lagos by police and brought to a detention centre. They were eventually let out and found a room with a family in a shantytown area.

A few months after this article was published, Minister for Justice Michael McDowell accused the media of having 'sought to create the impression that anyone who points out the true situation [of asylum seekers] is engaging in political racism … They refuse to address the very large abuse of asylum protection in Ireland. They claim to believe that it is wrong to point out what is happening lest it create prejudice against genuine asylum seekers. They are engaging in a form of verbal intimidation of those who would tell the truth.'[8] McDowell said the Irish Government's system of protecting asylum seekers was based on 'achieving a balance between fairness and firmness—fairness in ensuring that those genuinely in need of protection receive that protection quickly; firmness in dealing rigorously with abuses in our system which tie up resources which could be better utilised elsewhere.'[9]

In that same year the Department of Justice established the Irish Naturalisation and Immigration Service which it claimed would provide a 'one stop-shop' to centralise asylum, immigration, citizenship and visa services. The Government also launched a National Action Plan Against Racism as part of creating a more inclusive twenty-first century Ireland. 'Racism has no place in the Ireland of today,' wrote then Taoiseach Bertie Ahern in the introduction to the plan. 'The extent and pace of change in Ireland is clearly demonstrated by our transformation from a country of emigration to one of net inward migration. The emerging diversity of Irish society has the capacity to enrich all our communities and to make Ireland an example of best practice in promoting inclusion.'[10]

Magda Chmura, 2005

Magda Chmura was eighteen years old the day her life changed completely. The teenager was running for the school bus in her home village near Lublin in eastern Poland when she felt a searing pain in her head. She was late for school and tried to ignore the burning sensation pulsing through her skull as she caught up with the bus. 'I sat down on the seat beside my friend and told her I had a horrible headache. One of the women on the bus gave me some tablets, but when we were about half an hour away from school I asked my friend to call an ambulance.'

Magda's friend suggested she take the next bus home to her village and skip school, but Magda sensed the pain in her head was serious. The last thing she remembers is vomiting before losing consciousness. The eighteen-year-old woke up to discover she had suffered a brain aneurysm. Someone had called Magda's mother who was sitting beside her in the ambulance on the way to Lublin, a one hour journey from their home. 'It was very difficult for my mum. When she was six years old her mother had died so she had already gone through all that. She was crying for me and called my doctor, pleading with her to "please help my daughter". One of the arteries to my brain was damaged so the blood was pumping out. My mum said I looked horrible, that my face was all blue. They had to open up my head.'

Fortunately the doctors in Lublin were able to operate on Magda straight away, but the recovery period was a long and arduous process. 'I didn't go to school for three months and then there were another two months of summer holidays. I had always been a good student and I was one of the top in the class. But after the aneurysm I had a lot of difficulties with my concentration and couldn't understand anything. I couldn't do maths or learn English, it was horrible. When I read a word in English I could never remember it. I couldn't grasp things and struggled a lot.'

Aside from the learning difficulties, Magda also became increasingly depressed during her final year in secondary school. She says her faith and dedication to the Catholic Church served as a beacon of hope during those difficult months following the operation. 'I remember one year after the operation it was springtime and the grass was so green and beautiful. But I still felt down and depressed and was taking anti-depressants. I said a prayer and told God that if I didn't believe in him I would probably kill myself. My faith kept me going during that time. If I didn't believe in God, I don't know how it would have ended.' Her parents tried to help their daughter in every way they could in the year following the accident. However, they could not understand her depression. 'My family is a simple family, they didn't understand that their daughter could become so depressed after an operation. They wanted to do everything for me and helped me loads but they never completely understood.'

Magda remembers her childhood and teen years before her illness as a quiet but happy time. One of four children, she grew up on a farm near a village called Goscieradów. 'I can't imagine what it would be like to grow up in a city. I liked the feeling of freedom, of being on a farm. I think it's more natural for children.' As well as running the family farm, her father also inherited a small workshop where he built windowpanes. Despite his hard work on the farm, money was tight for the family and when Magda was fourteen her father had to move to Germany. 'To live in Poland only on farming is very difficult, especially when it's such a small farm. My father went to Germany for work and came home every month. It was like that for many years.'

Growing up under Communist rule in the 1980s, church attendance was very much frowned upon. However, Magda says the rules and restrictions around religion which applied in the cities often fell by the wayside in more rural areas. 'I suppose the faith in Polish villages was really strong. Every week you went to Mass and the religion lessons were taught in the church. My uncle was married in the church, not on a Sunday or Saturday, but quietly during the week. And his children were christened in the church. Of course his colleagues knew because they were all doing the same. The main message from the government may have been that Poland was a Communist country but people didn't care too much. They still went about their daily life. Everybody in our village went to church. My grandparents were very good in that way. They had a strong faith and I believe that because of that they led a good life.'

When Magda finished school she moved to the city of Kielce in central Poland to study economics. Her parents were initially nervous about letting their daughter move more than one-hundred kilometres away for her studies only eighteen months after her surgery. But Magda was eager to live in a city where she could meet new people and move on from her illness. Unfortunately, adjusting to her studies was not as easy as she had hoped. She had left behind a village where everyone knew she had suffered a brain aneurysm and moved to a university where no one had any idea what she had been through. Eager to teach her brain how to remember facts, figures and words, Magda joined the international students' association where she helped organise events. 'I was part of an organisation that did exchanges for international students so I became used to the idea of a global village, sharing your culture and living with different nationalities. I pushed myself more and more and ended up organising an international conference. I'd always liked organising things, it felt natural for me.'

Magda also volunteered with an NGO which encouraged young people to work abroad after graduation. She had considered applying for jobs in Poland but was still nervous about her ability to retain information in a work environment. She also knew that jobs in eastern Poland were difficult to find. 'In the back of my head I still believed I was not able for that work, that I would forget everything. It wasn't a confidence thing, it was just I knew I didn't have a good memory. I still don't know how I made it through college, but somehow I did it.' In 2004 Magda decided to follow the advice of her peers at the university NGO and signed up to take part in the European Voluntary Service programme. She applied to a number of countries across Europe and was selected to spend half a year in Ireland working with a youth support project in north Dublin. 'I didn't want to rely on my family so much, I wanted to be independent.'

Magda moved to Dublin and began working with children at an after-school club in Ballymun. She also helped teenagers and young mothers who took part in programmes at the club. She found a room in a house in Phibsborough and began attending the nearby St Peter's Catholic Church where she joined the choir. As her English improved, Magda began settling into her new Irish lifestyle. She was initially surprised by the sense of style she noticed around Dublin's streets. 'What struck me was that people didn't care what they were wearing. In Poland you are very conscious of your clothes and how you look. But there I was on the street, on a sunny day in Dublin, and I saw lots of women in leggings and short tops. They were all different shapes and sizes, skinny and fat. I couldn't believe that.'

After seven months in Ireland, Magda's placement in Ballymun came to an end and she moved back to Poland. She found a job in administration at the local secondary school in her village and moved back in with her parents. But she missed her Irish friends and the independence of living alone in Dublin. After seven months working at the school, she told her mother and father she was moving back to Ireland. 'My mum was worried at first and they both said not to go. They didn't want me to go to Ireland in the first place and they were worried about a young girl going away on her own. But the second time it was a bit easier because I was going to stay in my friend's house.'

Magda arrived back in Ireland in mid-2005 with €700 in her account, ready to find a job and build a new life for herself.

She spent a short while working at an accounting firm before finding a position with the revenue department at Ryanair. She liked working for the airline, but struggled to fully settle into the position and ended up moving to a job with ESB Networks. Magda quickly realised she had arrived into a country that was financially flourishing and at the peak of its boom years. Accustomed to the far more modest salaries across Poland—a nation still tentatively coming of age following the fall of the Berlin Wall—Magda was suddenly earning a sizeable income in a society eagerly embracing consumerism. 'It was a mad time and I became part of that madness. At first I was so enthusiastic about that way of life—the money, the trips, the restaurants, going to the shops every weekend buying tops and dresses. I was part of it, but so were lots of other people. I started to realise when I was buying all this stuff that I didn't actually need it and began asking what I really wanted from life. I started to search for what else I could do.'

In 2008 she witnessed the riches of the Celtic Tiger years fall to pieces with the economic crash. Fortunately Magda still had a job as a clerical officer, but was aware of the rapidly rising unemployment around her. 'Basically I started to notice people being more careful with their money. The lady who used to say she would never go to Aldi or Lidl and only did her shopping in Dunnes or Marks and Spencers was now shopping in Aldi. There was a feeling around that you should start saving.' She also felt a shift in the way Irish people spoke to and interacted with her. 'One person asked me "well, now that there's a downturn will you go back to Poland?" But I still had a job and was happy here. There was this perception that you should leave your job for Irish people. And I don't blame people for this. Ireland is for the Irish people mostly. It would be the same in Poland if loads of people from different countries arrived, they would probably react in the same way.'

As the years passed, Magda moved between a number of homes around the city. She struggled to build meaningful friendships with Poles, many of whom returned home after a few years in Ireland. 'Friendships were always fluctuating. If you move abroad and you don't have your family, you need friends. But my friends were always changing. Some people were going and some people were staying.' She did meet a number of Irish people through the local church choir. However, she worried that her strong opinions made her stand out from the crowd and eventually joined a Polish congregation. 'I'm very conservative. When I was in that choir I started to think the people didn't really share the same views and began to question myself.'

Magda says she understands why many people have chosen to move away from the Catholic Church in recent years. However, she feels conflicted by those who claim to be Catholic but who no longer attend Mass. 'In my view if you think you are a Catholic and you don't go to church, you have to ask yourself what kind of Catholic you are. You need to ask what do you believe in and what values would you like to follow. Europe was a Christian place, but now it's kind of losing its Christian roots and turning into a place with a lack of faith. I also think a big part of that is to do with the media. The media don't really support the Catholic faith or Catholic values. People are still searching for something, but they are turning to eastern religions and practices like Buddhism and yoga. I think there are still a lot of spiritual people out there who should come back to their Christian roots.'

After she moved to a new church, Magda started to become more involved in the Polish community in Ireland and developed an interest in Polish politics and history. She also helped set up an amateur theatre group in the new church. While she eventually lost interest in the debates around politics and history, she really enjoyed the theatre. 'I'd never done theatre before. When I was small in primary school I sang but I'd never acted. I don't particularly like the acting but what I do like is the organising. Once the group started doing some plays, the people who organised events started asking us to help out and get involved. In that way we organised a performance for the seventieth anniversary of the Warsaw Uprising. It was quite powerful to take part in that.'

After more than a decade in Ireland, Madga says she now has a mix of Irish friends—some from when she first moved here—and Polish friends. She recently bought a small apartment in Swords where her siblings, nieces and nephews can stay when they visit. She had grown tired of the constant stream of flatmates and decided the time had come to invest in her own property. And does Ireland feel more like home now that she owns an apartment here? 'I think Ireland became home a long time before I bought the apartment. Anyway, buying a place was never about calling Ireland my home. I was getting older and wanted some stability. I don't know if buying myself a house means I'm here for good because I don't know what will happen in the future. My home in Swords is lovely and quiet, it feels like a village really.'

She still struggles with the turnover of people arriving from and returning to Poland. 'People go home and you feel a bit lonely. I'm the kind of person who needs to live with someone in order to become friends. I'm not good at meeting people. I have a couple of friends in Swords but it's getting more difficult, especially when people have their own lives. I'm single but they have their own families.'

The results of the latest Irish census, held in April 2016, show that Polish people make up the largest group of foreign nationals living in Ireland, with 122,515 scattered across the country. However, just because Poles share a nationality does not mean they have the same interests, talents or professions, says Magda. 'Ireland's Polish community is divided into many different groups. I'm probably more part of the church community here, but there are many other kinds of groups. Obviously there are people with families and people without families. They're all into very different things. You can't generalise about them.'

Magda misses her family—all three of her siblings live close to home in Poland—and often invites them to visit her in Dublin. However, she says living abroad is much easier in 2017 than when she first moved here. 'Nowadays Europe is so small. You can sit on the plane and you're home in no time or you can go on Skype and see everyone. Sometimes it even feels weird that you're talking to your family on such a regular basis. When I came here in 2005 I was buying call cards all the time to ring my house in Poland.'

She says she's happy to stay in Ireland for now, but is reluctant to look too far into the future. 'It's very hard to say where you will be in the next five years because anything could happen. Also, because I'm single I'm not bound to anything. I own a house but I could sell it anytime. I'm independent and have whatever I need and want here. I have my life here. Maybe

I do get a bit lonely sometimes but that's why I get involved in lots of activities. Irish people have always been very good to me and because of this I feel like part of the community.

2006 Migration

'Recent times have seen a striking increase in public attention to migration ... events such as drowning of Africans in the Mediterranean and the Atlantic Ocean and terrorist threats have coloured debates and public perception. Coping with migration has become a serious challenge for the EU and its member states ... Global economic competition is growing and results in fears of job losses. Against this background of felt insecurity, the public presentation of immigrants and migratory phenomena by the media and by politicians is often biased or negative, linking them often almost exclusively to security issues.'[11]

The introductory paragraphs of this European Commission paper on the public perception of migration could easily have been written last week rather than eleven years ago. Drownings in the Mediterranean, terrorism-related security threats and negative portrayals of migrants are issues that continue to feature in daily news reports in 2017. A 2006 Human Rights Watch briefing warned that EU migration policies were largely focused on keeping migrants and asylum seekers out of the European Union, rather than introducing policies to protect the human rights of those forced to flee their homes. It reported that in 2006 the EU was pressing neighbouring states to take greater responsibility for migration and was committed to 'outsourcing' the control of migration, exactly what happened a decade later with the 2016 migrant deal between the EU and Turkey. 'Migration poses immense challenges for EU countries, both at home and abroad,' said Holly Cartner, Europe and Central Asia director at Human Rights Watch. 'But shirking responsibility for the rights of migrants and asylum seekers is not the answer.'[12]

In August 2006 the EU launched an operation to turn back small boats carrying migrants from Cape Verde, Mauritania and Senegal to the Spanish Canary Islands, which were struggling to cope with the influx of people arriving from West Africa. The European Commission's justice commissioner said he planned to ask EU member states to show more solidarity with Spain, increase the amount of money available for border control and strengthen the 'operational capacity' of the new EU border agency Frontex. The Canary Islands received more than 26,000 migrants during 2006, the vast majority arriving from Senegal. The European Commission described 2006 as a year of 'agenda setting with Africa' during which the EU and the African Union formulated a joint approach on migration for the first time. Recognising the urgent need to create more jobs and economic growth across Africa, the Commission promised dialogue and cooperation with North African countries to help manage migration more effectively and tackle the main push factors for people leaving their homes.

In Ireland, the debate around immigration had broadened to the question of children, specifically children who were arriving in the State unaccompanied or 'separated' from loved ones. In a 2006 report the Irish Refugee Council warned that rising numbers of unaccompanied children were being trafficked into the country and forced into a 'legal limbo' without asylum or protection. The Council wrote that more than 4,500 separated children had arrived in Ireland in recent years, the majority of them adolescents. It added that all children who came under the remit of the Irish State should be treated in a 'non-discriminatory manner' and their immigration status should not be a priority. 'The rights of separated children must go beyond vague aspirations,' it writes. 'The State has specific obligations to treat Irish and non-Irish children alike, providing an equality in care and benefits provision.'[13] The report also warned that 316 children who had arrived in the country as unaccompanied minors had gone missing and accused the public response to this news of not reflecting the seriousness of the problem. 'Some have responded that the reality of missing separated children is one of the vagaries of the asylum system. This is not a reasonable response.'

'Separated children—children outside their country of origin separated from parents or other caregivers—are invisible in Irish society,' wrote Héilean Rosenstock-Armie, Separated Children's Officer with the Irish Refugee Council in June of that year. 'This invisibility is twofold, first as children who often have no voice and, secondly, as asylum seekers marginalised in society. If these children are largely invisible in the first instance, who will notice if they go missing?' The existence of separated children in Ireland must force people to challenge their prejudices about migrants, wrote Rosenstock-Armie. Can we call them economic migrants, asylum shoppers or welfare fraudsters, she asked. 'Can the often blurred distinction between a coerced victim of trafficking and willing participant be applied to a child?'[14]

Responding to the report, Norah Gibbons, director of advocacy for Barnardo's, warned that children travelling to a foreign country without the protection of their parents were especially vulnerable to exploitation. 'The fact is, these children deserve the same consideration of care as their Irish counterparts, and the Irish State is failing in its duty of care to these children by not looking after them within our national acceptable limits of protection' she said. 'Children are vulnerable and children travelling to a foreign country without the protection of their parents are especially vulnerable to those who would seek to exploit them. We know from international research of the links between children who disappear and child trafficking.'[15]

That same year, the Department of Justice and An Garda Síochána produced a report on the legislation needed to deal with the problem of human trafficking. The report found that while Ireland was experiencing the trafficking of human beings on a much smaller scale than illegal immigration, it remained at similar risk from organised crime groups and networks as other EU nations. Despite the reportedly low numbers of people being trafficked into Ireland, the report warned that women from eastern European countries like Bulgaria, Romania and Lithuania were at particular risk of being trafficked into the country for sexual exploitation. It called for draft legislation to comply with the EU framework directive on combating trafficking in human beings and combating the sexual exploitation of children.

Fine Gael's Simon Coveney, then in opposition, called on the government to introduce temporary residency permits for people trafficked into Ireland for cheap labour or sexual exploitation. 'People who are trafficked are victims, and we should not lose sight of that fact,' said Mr Coveney. 'Human trafficking is rooted in poverty; the victims are usually women and they are forced into dangerous, illegal or abusive work.' Mr Coveney called for all EU member states to implement a Council Directive on reesidence permits so that people trafficked against their will could have the option of temporary residence. 'Women should not be deported immediately back to their countries of origin where their safety cannot be guaranteed. Very often they fear reprisals from the individuals that trafficked them. Instead, Ireland and other EU countries should consider granting these women periods of recovery and reflection.'[16]

2006 was also the year of the first Irish census to be held since the enlargement of the EU to twenty-five member states in 2004. Preliminary results released in July 2006 found there were 46,000 more immigrants than emigrants annually between 2002 and 2006 and reported that the population had increased by 318,000—an increase of 8% in four years—in the same time period, citing migration as the dominant factor for this growth. Some 250,000 migrant workers—mostly from Poland, Latvia, Slovakia and Lithuania—registered for Personal Public Service (PPS) numbers during 2005-2006 while a record monthly figure of 19,000 workers from new EU states registered to work in Ireland in July 2006. A total of 4,314 applications for asylum were submitted, marking a continued decrease in the number of applicants since a peak of 11,6334 in 2002. Some 5,527 people were living in the direct provision system by December 2006.

The Irish Times reported in August that the Government was considering a number of options—including appointing a minister of state with responsibility for integration—to help meet the needs of the rapidly-growing migrant population due to concerns around the provision of English language training for children at school and the high levels of unemployment among some groups of foreign nationals. The director of the Migrant Rights Centre of Ireland (MRCI), Siobhan O'Donoghue, said in July 2006 that Ireland's traditional understanding of Irish society, culture and traditions no longer sat comfortably alongside 'the growing realisation that we are not simply an isolated island off the mainland of Europe. Rather we are part of a Union bent on generating a collective regional identity'.[17]

Ms O'Donoghue warned that the Irish government's failure to acknowledge and adapt to the State's increasingly diverse and multicultural population could result in 'an increasingly fractured, tense, polarised and disenfranchised population, and will ultimately undermine governance and democracy … Ireland is at a crossroads and we are in the fortunate situation of being able to draw from a wealth of experience not only from other countries but also from work here in promoting social and economic inclusion, equality and in tackling racism. The integration of migrant workers and their families is not cost free, but the resources earmarked for it should be viewed as an essential investment in our future.'[18]

George Labbad, 2006

George Labbad always knew he would work in hospitality. As a child he was fascinated by the hard work and dedication that went into running his family's popular restaurant in the city of Aleppo. The bustling business, which employed nearly one hundred and eighty people, was always busy preparing for a seemingly never-ending stream of celebrations. In the morning and afternoon families would swim in the restaurant's large outdoor pool and lounge in deck chairs soaking up the warm sunshine. In the evenings tables and chairs were set up to serve Mediterranean dishes to hundreds of customers while live music played late into the night.

'The restaurant was like a landmark in the city,' says George as he flicks through photos of the venue on his phone. 'It could seat about eight hundred people and had been in the family since the late 1960s. I grew up there with the staff. Some of them had worked there since my grandfather opened it. Some were older than my dad, others the same age as him and then there were people my age. I wouldn't say I was the owner's son. I'd be working, moving chairs and tables. I'd be in the kitchen helping with whatever was needed. Or I'd be playing around and tasting the food!' George's parents dedicated their lives to the restaurant his grandfather first opened in 1969. As the eldest in the family, George, who is named after his grandfather, hoped to eventually take over the family business. 'There is this custom in Syria, I think it exists in Ireland too, where parents teach their son the business so they can pass it on. Of course I wanted to take over once they were ready.'

George remembers Aleppo as a thriving city which, before the war, had become a popular location for businesses, universities and schools. 'A big percentage of the Syrian economy came from Aleppo because of the factories in the city. They had opened the borders with Turkey so there was plenty of trade between the two countries. Aleppo was also very focused on hospitality and tourism. We appreciated guests coming to our homes and people visiting our city. Life was normal then. I had all my friends there, we went out for parties and had fun. It was probably one of the only cities that had a mixture of all the real life of Syrian society. You would have people with different religions and different beliefs all living under the same roof of that city. There was a strong gel that helped society stick together. It was a good civilisation, that's what Syria is all about.' This mix of people and religions could be seen among the staff at the La Gondole restaurant where a large number of the employees came from Kurdish backgrounds. 'Here in Ireland a couple of years back it was always Polish people working in restaurants, now it's more Brazilians. It was like that in Syria only it was Kurds who did the service industry jobs.'

George and his younger sister and brother were brought up in a Catholic household. His parents were eager for their children to speak fluent English and so, in 2001 when he was just a teenager, they sent George to Dublin for a two-month English language course. The summer camp was organised by the Marist Brothers in Clondalkin and offered classes to teenagers from around the world. George's parents originally planned to send their son to the UK but on the advice of a Marist brother in the children's school in Syria, they began investigating options in Ireland. 'In the end they decided to send me to Ireland over England because in the Irish school the teenagers stayed with host families. They wanted someone looking after me, that was the tipping point.'

In June 2001 George's parents brought him to the airport, waved goodbye and he set off on his first solo adventure abroad. 'When I arrived in Dublin airport all I knew was the name of the person who was coming to meet me. He was a brother from the school and had a really strong accent. I remember thinking there's no way I can understand what he's saying. I was still building up sentences in my head like "how's your day today?"'

George spent that first summer in Ireland learning English alongside students from countries like Spain, Italy and Argentina. He enjoyed the course so much that he kept coming back each year, spending every summer during his teen years in Dublin. After he finished school, he decided to stay in Syria and studied hospitality at university in Aleppo. However, he couldn't stop thinking about how much he wanted to return to his life in Dublin. He had kept in touch with the Marist brothers in Clondalkin, who offered to send him university prospectuses with listings of the courses on offer in the

Dublin Institute of Technology (DIT) and University College Dublin. 'I had looked at other options in the United States and Australia because we have extended family there but I felt comfortable in Ireland. I'd spent time there and knew there was a nice community.'

In 2006, George applied for a degree in International Management at the Dublin Institute of Technology and arrived in Ireland in late August of that year. On the recommendation of the Marist brothers, he found accommodation with a host family in Killiney who had rooms available for foreign students. 'They were an amazing family and I lived with them for two and half years. They really made an effort to look after me. They would take me to Howth on the weekends and we went to church together. The mother was almost like my own mum, always cooking what I wanted.'

Studying in a university with Irish students was an entirely different experience to spending two months with foreign teenagers in a language camp. 'I'd been in Ireland before so I had a hint of the culture but when you come to live in a place full time it's very different. You need to learn to go to the bank, the shop, how to buy your books and go to the library.' George also discovered very few Irish people had heard of Syria. When asked where he came from, he would describe his home as the large country beside Lebanon or below Turkey. 'No one knew about it then and it was hardly talked about. Then later it became very famous for all the wrong reasons.'

One month into his studies at DIT, George applied for a job at the five-star Westin Hotel in Dublin's city centre. What began as a part-time student placement turned into a more permanent position and after graduating from DIT he began working full time at the hotel. Each summer he would return home to visit his family and in 2010 his parents visited Dublin for their son's graduation and spent three weeks in the country. At that point, George's plan was still to return home to Aleppo and work in the family's restaurant. 'That trip was a very happy time for my parents. Their son was graduating from university and they could be in Ireland for the ceremony. After that they went back to Syria and continued their life. They had a restaurant to run.'

Shortly after their visit, news began filtering through the media of the violence breaking out across Syria. 'Before then I wasn't interested in hearing the news. I preferred reading articles in travel or hospitality magazines about plans to open new hotels and restaurants. But then things suddenly changed and I started reading the news and checking Arabic websites all the time. I called my parents on a daily basis through Skype just to check they were OK.'

In July 2012 the conflict in Syria hit Aleppo. That same month, on 7 July, the Labbads' restaurant hosted a concert with the internationally renowned Arab singer Nassif Zeytoun who performed for more than 1,800 people. Less than three weeks later, the restaurant was closed. 'Everything my parents wanted in their life and worked for was in that restaurant. And then suddenly, it was gone. Can you imagine working for a place for over 30 years, sacrificing everything for it and then suddenly, it's no more? They couldn't take a fork or glass with them when they left. Their stores were massively packed with supplies, drinks and food. All their capital was in those stores.' Only two years previously, George's parents had invested all their savings in the renovation and expansion of the restaurant. 'They had created a new seating area, replenished the swimming pool, everything. It was the boom time, very similar to the Celtic Tiger here. Everyone was telling them you have the money, you should expand.'

Once the violence hit the outskirts of Aleppo, George's parents were unable to reach the restaurant. With rebel groups attacking the government-run centre of the city, it was far too dangerous for any staff member to approach the property. 'There were hotspots across the city, like frontlines where the two sides were fighting. The restaurant was on one of those frontlines. Let's say the restaurant is in Blackrock and suddenly all of Ballsbridge closes down and you can't get through. You're just locked in this circle.'

Back in Ireland, George was struggling to understand why his parents were unable to reach their business. 'It had become a no-go area but from my end I kept asking, what do you mean? Why can't you just go there and bring back what you can? They told me no, it's right on the frontline. I don't know how to describe that time, I can't. I went days without sleeping. It was so hard to believe what was happening and to take it all in. There was also the fear of what was coming.'

Unable to rely on savings to support the whole family, George's parents opened a coffee shop in the city centre where they employed a small number of staff from the restaurant. He says his father's goal in running La Gondole was never to make millions but to protect the welfare of his employees who numbered more than 200 people. He knew its closure had left hundreds of families in dire financial straits. 'My dad's work ethic was always about the people. When he thought about the restaurant it wasn't about making $1 million or $2 million, it was about providing life for hundreds of families. The staff at the restaurant was made up of families. You'd see ten people working there who were all somehow related. It's not like here, you didn't hire and then fire someone. These were people you kept. If he didn't work as a waiter, you'd put him in the kitchen. You'd help the person until he found the right job.'

Back in Ireland, George was frantically worrying about his parents and siblings. 'It was about getting to speak to them on Skype each day. There was only one hour of electricity and if we missed that, we'd have to talk the next day. When I was at work there were so many thoughts crossing my mind; are they OK? What's happened today? Those two years were terrible. Each morning I would wake up and think, will I get that call with the bad news?'

In 2014, George read a news report about the Irish Government's decision to introduce the Syrian Humanitarian Admission Programme (SHAP) under which Syrians already living in Ireland could apply for their family to join them. With the guidance of the Crosscare support agency, George applied for his parents and younger brother and sister to come to Ireland. His application was accepted and the family arrived in February 2015. He had not seen them in four and a half years. 'For my parents the main thing was for my brother and sister to get out. They didn't really care about themselves. But even when you're in your twenties you still need support from your parents. Think of all the people here in Ireland in their thirties who are still living with their parents. Just because you're an adult doesn't mean you don't need your family around you. I went to the airport to meet them and it was very emotional.

I'd seen my parents when they visited for my graduation but I hadn't seen my brother or sister in years. The last time I'd seen my brother he was sixteen, now he was twenty. I'd missed those critical four years and saw a different person in the airport. He was taller than me and had a beard. He was an adult.'

George's parents are now living in an apartment in Dublin close to his home. Under the SHAP programme the family are entitled to work but are not eligible for social welfare. His sister, who already spoke good English, is working in retail in Dundrum in south Dublin while his twenty-one-year-old brother, who recently graduated from secondary school, is working as a chef. His parents, who spoke very little English on arrival, are still taking English classes while the three siblings support the family through their work. 'My sister and I only have a gap of three years so we are very close and always laugh together. I'm also so happy my brother is here because I get to spend time with him. The gap in our ages makes me feel like he's almost my own child so I want to look after him. He needs to have a good life and I will support him all the way.'

Even though his mother's English has improved, George knows his parents are struggling to settle into life in Ireland and that they desperately miss friends and family in Syria. 'It's getting better for my mum but she's homesick, just like any of us. She's tried to volunteer in workshops and goes to the library. I'm trying to use my free time to help them find activities they can get involved in. The main thing when someone moves here is to integrate and to get more involved.' George prefers not to speak with his family about the restaurant back in Aleppo—he knows how difficult it is for his parents to reflect on everything they've lost. 'My dad used to work there all day, from 8am-8pm.

Sometimes he would work twenty hours straight into the night. It was everything for him. Even now, I would not want to open that subject with him.'

2019 will mark sixty years since the restaurant opened and George still hopes the family will be able to celebrate the anniversary. 'I've learned a lot more about anniversaries here and they are critical points. It's something I want to do for my family and I'm passionate about.' Like most Syrians who have been forced to leave their homes, he knows his parents still dream of the day when they can return home to Aleppo. 'Syrians in general, regardless of the way they left the country or their opinions about the war, regardless of which side they're on, they all say they'd love to go back to the life they used to have. They want to go back home to their street and their friends. Everyone usually looks to the future but I suppose now for Syrians, unfortunately they're looking at the past. People have left the country but they will never really leave. They're still linked to that place big time.'

George is very happy to live in Ireland. However, he misses life in Syria before the war and the days when he used to dream about his future in Aleppo. 'I never lived there during the war so for me, I'm missing the time when you would go back and everyone was together. But now everyone has left. I miss somewhere that doesn't exist anymore. The streets are still there but the people are somewhere else. And even if you try to reunite and get together by holding reunions somewhere else in the world, it will never feel the same. It was home.' After more than a decade in Ireland, George says Dublin now also feels like home. He manages the operations at the front desk of the Westin Hotel and dreams of becoming the general manager of a hotel one day. He loves interacting with people through his work and finds it funny when tourists ask about his name. 'When I tell someone I'm from Syria they ask how long I've been here and tell me I'm so lucky to be in Ireland. Then they'll ask my name and I say George. They ask, "no, what's your real name?" Again, I say George. I'm very proud to tell them I'm Christian and from Syria.'

George still thinks of his home country as a diverse nation and longs for the day when he can return to a Syria where people live alongside each other in peace, despite any differences in opinion. 'I can't force my opinion on you and you're not supposed to force yours on me. It's about how you treat people and respect others. Whether they believe in God or not, whether they are Muslims or Christians or whatever, if you respect them, they will respect you back. Here in Ireland we talk about LGBT rights but in Syria that was a hidden area. I've been thinking about it more now that I live here and realise you have to accept everyone in society. That's what makes us bigger and stronger, it's what humanity is all about. That's the part we missed in Syria and that created the war.'

He says Syrians seeking asylum in countries like Ireland must make the effort to integrate into European society. 'I came here at a young age which made it easier to integrate. I'm thirty years old now and I've spent twelve years here so it really does feel like I belong. The only way to feel like you really belong is through memories—through your work, your friends, the streets that you have walked in. I have all that here. I'm always going to live here regardless of what happens in Syria. I'm not going to leave the contact I've built here. I have memories here now.'

2007 Migration

In 2007 applications for asylum in Ireland dropped to their lowest point since 1997. While EU migrants from Central and Eastern Europe continued to arrive in their droves, the number of applications for asylum fell to just 3,985, down from 11,634 applications in 2002. Peter O'Mahony, former chief executive of the Irish Refugee Council, said at the time that Ireland had been given 'a window of opportunity' to ensure immigrants were encouraged and enabled to integrate into Irish society. 'If we fail to take the right initiatives, the window will soon have slammed shut. If that happens, the recent experience of countries such as the Netherlands and France would suggest that disaffection among marginalised migrant communities and their descendants in Ireland might grow to dangerous levels with unknown but negative consequences for society at large.'[19]

Despite this drop in asylum seekers, the economic migrants kept coming. The 2006 census revealed that the number of Polish arrivals had escalated significantly since the 2002 census, with 63,267 Poles living in Ireland, compared to 2,124 in 2002; 24,628 Lithuanians, compared to 2,104, and 13,319 Latvians, compared to 1,797. However, Minister of State for Integration Conor Lenihan, who was appointed to this newly created position following the 2007 general election, argued that the 2006 census results seriously underestimated the number of foreigners living in Ireland, claiming that non-Irish nationals could actually make up 13-15% of the population (the census reported non-Irish nationals accounted for 10% of the population).

Dr Steven Loyal, a UCD sociologist, wrote in August that migrants had made a 'major contribution' to Ireland's economic growth, 'taking jobs no one else will do, as well as higher occupations others in Ireland cannot do'. 'It is time Ireland stopped talking about integration and inter-culturalism and actually started doing something to make them a reality. That entails language classes, allowing family reunification, easier pathways to citizenship and enforcing anti-discrimination laws.'[20]

Meanwhile, internationally, migration was re-emerging as a key issue. The United Nations Refugee Agency (UNHCR) reported in November 2006 that Iraq was 'haemorrhaging' people and that the humanitarian crisis the world feared when war broke out in 2003 had truly begun unfolding. The agency estimated in December 2007 that at least 2.4 million Iraqis were internally displaced with at least another 2.2 million in neighbouring states, most of them in Syria and Jordan. As estimated 1.5 million people fled to Syria seeking asylum while over half a million travelled to Jordan.

Human Rights Watch warned that the Iraqi displacement crisis showed 'no signs of abating' with tens of thousands of Iraqis continuing to leave their homes each month. The agency added that Iraq's neighbours, tired of watching hundreds of thousands of asylum seekers flowing over their borders, were closing off escape routes for those fleeing the conflict. Jordan and Egypt effectively closed their doors to refugees, while Saudi Arabia announced it was building a 900km border security fence to keep out 'smugglers, terrorists, and Iraqi refugees'. Human Rights Watch warned that the responsibility to provide and maintain asylum for Iraqi refugees could not rest solely on countries that border Iraq. It stressed that the United States and the UK, who had led the 2003 invasion of Iraq, 'have a humanitarian responsibility both to refugees living in the region and to those still seeking refuge.'[21]

In Europe, anti-immigrant sentiment was growing. In Switzerland, as voters prepared to go to the polls in the October general election, a campaign poster appeared across the country aimed at deporting foreigners who had committed crimes. It showed three white sheep kicking a black sheep against a backdrop of the Swiss flag, and was produced by the anti-immigrant People's Party (SVP) which went on to enjoy its best showing ever in a Swiss election with 29% of the vote. *The New York Times* wrote that the party's underlying message had 'polarised a country that prides itself on peaceful consensus in politics, neutrality in foreign policy and tolerance in human relations.'[22]

Conversely, just over the border in Germany, measures were being introduced to promote the integration of migrants. These included increasing the maximum number of hours of German language classes for immigrants from six hundred to nine hundred, imposing financial penalties on immigrants not turning up for classes, and providing female-only language courses for Muslim women. In March 2007 Chancellor Angela Merkel called for a comprehensive, systematic approach to the country's integration policy. 'Integration does not take place automatically and cannot merely be superimposed from above,' she said. 'Our society will become richer and more humane through tolerance and open-mindedness. Integration is a topic which concerns us all—people from migrant families as well as citizens who are long-term residents. Integration can only succeed in cooperation. It is our task to be able to perceive and experience our common house Germany as a likeable and liveable home.'

A year later Conor Lenihan would launch a similar document entitled *Migration Nation* which called for an Irish approach to integration focusing on the role of local communities, local authorities, sporting bodies, faith based groups and political parties. He quoted the then President Mary McAleese by calling on the Irish people to draw from the nation's common experience of migration and exile. 'We have recent memory of the loneliness, the sense of failure evoked by our inability to provide for our own people and the courage it took to start a new life far from home.'[23]

Irish people arguably feel this common experience of displacement more strongly that most other western European nations, and this made it easy for them during a period of unprecedented prosperity to pledge support to those fleeing persecution and poverty. However, in the months and years that followed, as the nation plunged into a period of deep economic instability, that desire to help the 'other', from a far off, unknown land, would become increasingly challenging for the citizens of this country.

Azeez Yusuff, 2007

Before Azeez Yusuff moved to Ireland ten years ago he had never seen a white person. For this young boy from Nigeria, people with white skin belonged in TV soaps and Hollywood movies. They did not fit into the daily life of his childhood growing up in a bustling Nigerian city. The first time he saw a white person in the flesh was at the airport in Lagos shortly before he and his older brother boarded their flight en route to Ireland. 'I had never seen any white people or foreigners before and they looked so strange. I'd see them on telly but never in real life. Before that, if we ever travelled it was only an hour away from home to see our cousins. But in the airport there were a few white people and I was like wow. What is going on?'

Azeez was just eleven years old when he stepped onto a plane for the first time and flew to Ireland to join his parents. He can still remember the fear of sitting in a large mechanical object while praying it would not fall out of the sky. He was also confused about where he and his brother were going and why they were leaving friends and family behind. All their grandmother had told them was they were going on a trip. 'I still remember the moment she said it. It was during the Eid celebrations when the whole family would come together. I was helping with the cooking and she suddenly said we were going away. I was surprised because Ramadan is always spent with the family. She said we had to dress up in our best clothes and then took us to airport. They tried to keep the whole thing secret.'

Azeez's father left Nigeria to look for work abroad when his youngest son was one year old. When Azeez was five, his mother also left. 'What they were doing was looking for better opportunities for us. Back home education is key and they wanted us to have more options. When my dad left I was so young that it just felt normal that he'd gone for work. My mum would say he was coming back in a few months but then months turned into years. Obviously with your mum you have a special relationship. If she had told me she was leaving for a year I wouldn't have let her go. I was really close to her, such a mummy's boy. I still am even though I'm twenty-two. I always talk to her.'

Unbeknown to Azeez and his brother at the time, his mother was travelling to Ireland to join his father who had applied for asylum and was living in a direct provision centre in Dublin. The couple were placed in a centre together and spent the next few years waiting for their papers to come through. As soon as they were given leave to remain, they found jobs as cleaners and made arrangements for their two young sons to join them in Ireland. 'We are really grateful for what they did for us. Everything they sacrificed and they went through, that was all for their kids. I've come to realise this over time and it's really stayed with me. They wanted to make sure everything was OK before they brought us over. Obviously we didn't know anything about this until we arrived here.'

Leaving their grandmother in Nigeria was very difficult for the two boys. They had moved into her home in the city of Ibadan, north of Lagos, after their mother left and developed a strong bond with her. 'My grandma is like another mum. After my mum left, she was always there for us. When we left Nigeria it was very hard for all of us but in a way she was happy too. She wanted us to be with our parents because she always told us there was nothing better than a mother's love. It was really difficult leaving her behind but we still talk. The way I think about it is that in order to move on in life you have to make some sacrifices.'

At Dublin Airport he was greeted by his mother whom he had not seen in six years and his father, who had been gone most of his life. 'I remember it was freezing when I arrived in Ireland. It was February and so cold. I hadn't seen my parents in a long time. It was a crazy feeling but it was one of the best days of my life.' Azeez's parents had found a home in Tallaght in south Dublin and enrolled their two sons in sixth class at the local primary school. However, his mother worried that the brothers might not mix with the other boys in the class if they stuck together so requested that Azeez be moved into fifth class.

'It was definitely a clever decision because obviously you would stay with your brother and it would be more comfortable. But when she told me about the move I was mad at first. I didn't know who I could talk to. I really stood out in class—that was scary.' While Azeez had already learned English at school in Nigeria, he was used to speaking Yoruba at home and with his friends. 'Obviously the language barrier was really difficult in terms of not understanding people. In

Nigeria, English is the first language but it's not what you speak normally. I spoke Yoruba, that's my language. I had basic English but people spoke so fast. How could I catch up with that? In Nigeria I had an identity but when I came here I didn't have one anymore. Back home I knew people in school but over here I just felt left out. I had been the loud guy in class but here I couldn't even speak the language or make friends. I know people struggle to believe that now because I'm a big guy. But back then everyone in the class was Irish born and I really stood out. People already had their own circle of friends. It was just me by myself. It was very scary and I would go home bawling crying.'

By sixth class Azeez was being bullied by classmates at school. However, one day a boy came over and started talking to him. 'After he saw me getting bullied he sat down beside me and we just talked. Even though I didn't really understand what he was saying and he didn't understand me, he decided to help me. I made friends with that guy and after that everything just became easier because he was so welcoming and had loads of friends. It was very big of him and we're still friends today.' With the support of this new group of friends, along with his increasingly fluent English, Azeez began secondary school with a new-found confidence and sense of self. However, he quickly fell in with what he describes as the wrong crowd. 'The gang I was hanging around with was always getting in trouble. In first and second year the teachers definitely didn't like me because my attitude stank.'

It was around this time that Azeez's father suggested his son join the local Marks Celtic football club to make friends and keep improving his English. The thirteen-year-old quickly discovered he had a talent for the game and found his speed helped him stand out in the team. In third year of school he became friendly with a boy called Abdul who played with the same club. Abdul was also a member of the Sports Against Racism Ireland (SARI) organisation, which uses sport to promote social inclusion, and encouraged Azeez to get involved. 'He introduced me to SARI and showed me what I could really get out of sports. Before that I thought football was just for fun. But I found out that with youth development, it could really break down walls and create change. I started their weekly soccer nights programme where I met so many people from different cultures and religions. I realised it was unique.'

As Azeez spent more time volunteering with SARI, he began reflecting on his gang at school and his behaviour in class. 'The group I used to hang around with got in trouble a lot and that definitely influenced me. I got suspended once for fighting in school. That's when I came to my senses. I didn't like the way I was going. I decided to do Transition Year and not go straight into fifth year with the group. Thank God I did that.'

Azeez set himself the goal of winning the school's sports person of the year award which he achieved in his final year. He continued playing soccer and moved around a number of teams in Castleknock, Crumlin and Cherry Orchard. He was then invited to join the Shamrock Rovers under 19s team. Unfortunately, after two years playing with Shamrock Rovers, Azeez was forced to take a break after he sustained a knee injury and had to undergo surgery. After the operation, his friend Abdul suggested he could stay involved with the sport by coaching the newly formed Muslim women's soccer team in Dublin. Diverse City FC had been established by a group of young Dubliners after FIFA lifted the ban on headscarves during matches and they were looking for a coach to lead their training sessions in Phoenix Park. 'I absolutely loved coaching Diverse City. What I've found is a lot of women don't really get involved in sport, but with Diverse City it's totally different. It doesn't matter if you're really good at football. Anyone can come along and we help them develop their skills. Soccer is a physical activity that is key for everybody, it doesn't matter if you're a boy or a girl.'

Azeez is still recovering from his knee injury but hopes to return to play with Shamrock Rovers in the future. 'I wasn't with the club for a long time, but I'm proud I played with them. I'm still training but I can't focus on football right now because my knee's not stable enough. My goal is to play in the premier division in the Airtricity league, but right now I need to focus on college.'

Asked why soccer continues to play such an important role in his life, Azeez says it comes down to feeling relaxed and happy. 'I've discovered that sport releases all the stress from my body. When I play I literally drop everything. I don't think of college work, family problems, nothing. I just focus on playing and after I finish I feel so happy on the pitch. When I play football, I can just leave any problem I have aside and focus on the game. When you join a club you definitely build relationships and meet people you can trust and talk to. I don't like keeping things inside because it just creates a negative energy. For new people who are coming into the country, my advice is to definitely join clubs or societies. It doesn't have to be sport, but it really has opened a lot of doors for me.'

Azeez has passed this love of sport on to his younger siblings who were born in Ireland after he moved from Nigeria. His younger brother plays soccer for Knocklyon FC in Dublin and his two younger sisters play Gaelic football and camogie. He also enjoys playing Gaelic football. 'I like the fitness aspect of it. It's much more physical than soccer and I think the training is more challenging.'

Azeez is now in his final year of computer science at the National College of Ireland, specialising in cyber security. After graduation he hopes to find a job that will allow him to combine his interest in sport with his expertise in computer science. 'I think I might also do a degree in personal training. With my computer science degree I can develop websites, but sports will always be the main focus for me.' Despite the demands of college work, the twenty-two-year-old continues to coach the young women who play with Diverse City. He is now head coach with SARI and often gives workshops about diversity and integration in Ireland. 'I do a workshop on acceptance and I tell them my story about that one guy who helped me out in sixth class. I use that example of the person who helped change my life a lot. I'm in college now, I've travelled to nearly twenty countries and I believe it all comes down to that one boy who helped me out.'

Azeez has represented SARI at conferences around Europe, meeting with refugee support groups in France, Luxembourg, Germany, Belgium, the UK and Spain to discuss the importance of sport in promoting integration. 'Take for example football. It doesn't matter what language you speak or where you're from. The only thing that matters is that you understand the rules of football. It allows people to communicate in a way they never did before, while also having fun. It brings people together, that's the world of sport.'

Azeez admits there's still a lot of work to be done around acceptance of and understanding different cultures in Ireland. When he first arrived here more than a decade ago, he often experienced racism on the streets. 'People would use the n-word and say "you're black, go back to your country".' While he no longer experiences this level of racism on a daily basis, he is often targeted when he walks to the Mosque on a Friday dressed in the traditional jalabiya garment. 'You get people staring at you and saying things about Isis. I just ignore it. In fact, if someone says that I try to talk to them to see it from their perspective. I try to reason with people if I don't understand why they behave in that way. I'd actually really like to meet that person and have a one-on-one conversation just to see where he's coming from. The way I see it, we only have a few people whose minds work in this way. But if we don't fully understand the problem we can't find a solution.'

Azeez has never felt threatened by this rejection of his Muslim beliefs, but often fears for his mother and sisters. 'I'm not that scared by it but the people I am worried about are Muslim women like my little sisters and my mum. They wear the hijab and people can see they are Muslim. It's scary because you hear in England of people throwing acid at people on the streets. I've told my little sisters to be careful and if there's any problem just call me. It's tough and it's not fair on them, not at all.' Azeez also worries that the African-Irish and white Irish living in areas like Tallaght are not making a strong enough effort to mix and get to know one another. 'In terms of sport I think I can help and am planning to hold a tournament there. I'm trying to train local people and get three or four leaders from the young people to help me out.' The key, says Azeez, is convincing people to continue hanging out together after the soccer tournament has finished. 'Sport can definitely unite people but my question is what can we do to keep them together? That's the next step.'

The international meetings he has attended through SARI give him the chance to discuss these barriers to integration with young people from abroad. 'At the youth exchanges you get people from other countries coming up with their own ideas and bringing different experiences. With every trip that's what we're trying to do. I still have a lot to learn about this myself. Knowledge never stops.'

Aside from sport and college, the main event on Azeez's mind is his family's upcoming trip to Nigeria. It will be his first time back in Africa since he and his brother left in 2007. He will also see his grandmother for the first time in more than ten years. 'I'm really excited and a little nervous too I guess. I've talked to my grandmother on the phone, but it's going to be so different when I see her. I can't describe how I'm really feeling about seeing a person I haven't seen in such a long time. I can't wait.'

After more than a decade living in Ireland, Azeez says he feels Irish. 'When people ask where I am from I tell them I'm originally from Nigeria but that I'm Irish. Obviously I was born in Nigeria, but I've lived here longer than I lived in Nigeria. This is my home, my friends are here. Here is where I made myself and it's where everything has happened for me. And I'm not done yet, I still have lots of things to achieve and am looking forward to it. I'm Nigerian and I'm proud to be Nigerian, but I'm Irish in my blood.'

He is grateful for the support over the years from his older brother, who now works as a carer in a Dublin hospital. 'Back home we fought a lot but he actually understood what was going on with my parents. He had to mature really quickly. If ever I cried in Nigeria he would say "it's gonna be OK, they're coming back." I really appreciate everything he's done for me.'

Azeez's main goal once he graduates from college is to make enough money to allow his parents to retire from their work. His mother now works as a kitchen assistant and his father as a security guard, but he wants to give them the chance to relax and finally enjoy life. 'To be honest, everything I'm doing right now in terms of SARI and college, I'm doing it for them. I want to give them something back because of the struggle they went through for me. That's my ambition, to get a degree and help them out.'

2008 Migration

In 2008 the tectonic plates of the rich world's economy started to shift. 'So real and massive was the threat that governments began planning for the social disorder that would follow as even basic payments systems broke down', wrote economist Dan O'Brien. 'The downturn was deep enough to be named the Great Recession. However, as with other recessions caused by financial collapses, there was never going to be a quick recovery from the crash of 2008.'[24]

Between 2008 and 2009 Ireland experienced one of the most acute economic downturns in the industrialised world, with gross national product falling by nearly 14%. The impact of this financial and economic collapse on immigrant communities was substantial. In the decade leading up to 2008, booming economies across Western Europe had created plenty of opportunities for millions of job seekers but with the arrival of a recession, European governments rapidly changed their minds about the benefits of immigration. Spain, a country which in 2005 had legalised 560,000 immigrants from Latin American and North Africa, announced a voluntary return programme to give unemployed, legally resident migrants the chance to return home. Even before the banking crisis hit, the European Parliament had approved a directive encouraging unauthorised immigrants to go back to their countries of origin.

In Ireland immigrants were far more likely to find themselves without work in the aftermath of the financial crash. In 2008, non-Irish nationals accounted for 11.5% of the population with people from the United States and Nigeria making up the two largest non-Irish nationalities in Ireland. The number of immigrants arriving in Ireland fell by 28% to 63,927 while the number of emigrants rose by more than 40%. A total of 3,866 asylum applications were received in 2008, a 2.9% decrease on the previous year. The top nationalities to apply for asylum were Nigeria, Pakistan, Iraq, Georgia and China. There were a total of 7,214 people living in direct provision centres in December 2008.

By the end of 2008 the unemployment rate for non-Irish nationals was 9.5% compared to 7.3% for Irish nationals with immigrants working in the construction, retail and hospitality sectors suffering significant job losses. The Economic and Social Research Institute (ESRI) noted that immigrant communities were 'impacted heavily' by job cuts in 2008 and faced 'lower wages and occupational downgrading'.[25] Support programmes for migrants also took an immediate hit and funding for the Office of the Minister for Integration was cut by more than a quarter.

Before the crash even happened, immigrants in Ireland were experiencing a new wave of negativity in the run up to the first referendum on the Lisbon Treaty in June, which was defeated by a margin of 53.4% to 46.6%. Research carried out by the European Commission in the days following the referendum found that immigration was 'an unspoken factor' in the No vote, with voters expressing real concern at the influx of immigrants to Ireland. Meanwhile a national debate around discrimination by immigration officers at Dublin Airport blew up mid-2008 after a number of visitors complained that immigration procedures at ports of entry were 'arbitrary' and heavy-handed. Two of the most high profile cases were of an Indian man who had won a trip to Ireland through a Tourism Ireland event but claimed to have experienced 'harassment and racial discrimination' at Dublin airport; and a Nigerian priest who was refused leave to land, arrested, strip-searched and placed overnight in a prison cell despite holding a valid tourist visa.

Internationally, the treatment of immigrants was not much better. In the United States the government was planning to erect more than one thousand miles of fencing along its border with Mexico in its clamp down on illegal immigration and drug smuggling. When Barack Obama won the presidential election in November 2008 many hundreds of thousands of undocumented migrants hoped the first black president of the United States, and the son of a Kenyan immigrant, would help them find a path to legalisation. Migrant policy had played a prominent role in the Obama campaign during the primary elections and in March 2007 the future president said it was 'absolutely vital' to bring millions of undocumented workers 'out of the shadows and give them the opportunity to travel a pathway to citizenship'.

In Europe, restrictions on asylum seekers arriving across southern borders were becoming increasingly common with Frontex, the European Border and Coast Guard Agency, continuing their patrols of the Mediterranean on the lookout for boats attempting to cross to the EU. Philippe Legrain, author of *Immigrants: Your Country Needs Them,* wrote in August 2008 that Europe's clampdown on immigration was 'neither fair nor sensible'. Legrain rejected the EU's new return directive which allowed governments to detain unauthorised migrants for up to 18 months and criticised French president Nicolas Sarkozy, the son of a Hungarian migrant, for his calls to expel more illegal migrants and beef up policing on the EU borders. Writing in *The Guardian* in 2008, Legrain noted:

> 'Undocumented migrants are not criminals, nor are they an invading army ... They are human beings less fortunate than ourselves. Most come to do jobs that comfortable Europeans no longer want to do, but as Europe's front doors are closed, they have to creep in through the back. Far from threatening Europe's ageing societies, they are reinvigorating them ... Europe's increasingly costly border controls fail to keep foreigners out. Instead, they foster people-smuggling and an ever-expanding shadow economy in which illegal migrants are vulnerable to exploitation, labour laws are broken and taxes go unpaid.'[26]

Legrain wrote these words just weeks before the world's banking system collapsed. Any calls to 'tear down walls' in the aftermath of the financial crash mostly fell on deaf ears. Many of those who had supported the arrival of migrants during times of prosperity fell silent. Focus now turned to our own jobs and our own homes. Much of the empathy and compassion towards migrants crossing the Mediterranean disintegrated as the citizens of the Western World buckled down to weather the storm of the Great Recession.

Tibor and Aniko Szabo, 2008

Tibor Szabo still has the one euro coin the Aircoach driver gave him as change the night he and his girlfriend Aniko arrived in Dublin. The Hungarian nurse hangs onto the money from that first bus fare as a reminder of how he felt arriving on this small western European island. Before coming to Ireland, Tibor had spent eight years working two jobs as a nurse to make ends meet and felt he was at a dead end in his career. 'I couldn't see any escape from it. I was working in an intensive care unit and on a home care team. If I had stayed in Hungary I might have achieved things professionally but in terms of finances it was too difficult. A registered nurse working in ICU would earn about €450-€550 per month. The cost of living is less in Hungary than here, however it was still not enough to live on.'

It was Aniko who suggested Tibor try applying for a job as an air steward. She had read an advertisement from an Irish airline in the paper calling for Hungarian applicants and encouraged her boyfriend to send in an application. 'I'd always loved flying and travelling and I thought I could use some of my healthcare experience if one of the passengers was sick,' remembers Tibor. 'I went to the capital and did the interview through English but for some reason I never heard back. After that I asked myself why did I want to change my profession. I already had nursing and it was perfect for me.' His meeting with the Irish airline gave Tibor the idea to investigate healthcare opportunities in Ireland. 'It was 2006 and Ireland was doing quite well. I only spoke English so that restricted me to a few countries around the world. The United States was too far; Australia was even further, so that left the UK and Ireland. I did research from home and from the library into Ireland and thought this country might work out.'

Growing up in Hungary in the 1980s, students had to learn Russian rather than English. It was only later, after the fall of the Berlin Wall in 1989, that English classes became more widely available in Hungarian schools. Tibor was thirteen years old when Communist rule in the Hungarian People's Republic came to an end. 'I still remember that year. The teachers in school had started saying it was an important event and that we needed to pay attention. I suppose they wanted to open our eyes to what was happening outside our town. But there was never any aggression or fear. I think people were actually relieved that there was a new ideology coming on board that would make a difference. That generation of teachers and parents, they had seen enough whereas I hadn't seen the half of it. After 1989, I think the whole interest towards political life, even for youngsters like me, was interesting because of the new faces, the new voices and the new ideas.'

While Tibor was finally able to learn English after 1989, he was not happy with the quality of teaching and decided to pay for private lessons when he began his nursing degree at university. 'For further education you need to have another language, that was my primary goal. But after a few years I just found it interesting to speak English. It was opening up so many doors for me so I decided to invest a bit more time and money into it.' He says his decision to become a nurse was most likely influenced by his mother who worked as the director of nursing in a hospital for decades. 'I think the work suited me because I have an aptitude towards helping people in trouble. I find it easy just to listen to them. I think that's the first thing I realised, that when I was sitting with someone I enjoyed talking to them. I'm a tiny bit shy and don't really like to open up so I just let other people talk.'

Aniko, who is also a nurse, says she knew from the age of six that she wanted to work in healthcare. 'At first I wanted to be a dentist but I was not clever enough to go to dentistry school. I still knew I wanted to work in health and that I liked helping people.' The couple met while they were both working in a hospital in the city of Szeged in southern Hungary. They had been together for two years when Tibor began making arrangements to move to Ireland. By that point he had completed a course in translating biology terms from Hungarian to English so moving to an English-speaking country felt like the next logical step if he wanted to develop his career abroad.

It took Tibor a year to complete the complicated registration process that would enable him to work as a nurse in Ireland. Once the registration was confirmed he sent his CV to recruitment agencies in Dublin and soon after received word that a new private hospital called the Beacon in Dublin wanted to interview him over Skype. A few days after the interview they called back with a job offer. Even though Aniko only spoke basic English, she decided to go with her boyfriend in the hope that she could attend a language school in Dublin before applying for work in a hospital. 'I was very bad at English at that time. I kind of understood what the people around me were saying but if it was a phone conversation it was a struggle. I had studied Italian at school and only had two years of English.'

In April 2008 the couple boarded a plane for Dublin where Tibor was to begin his new job as a nurse in the Beacon's oncology unit. The hospital paid for two week's accommodation while they looked for somewhere more permanent to live. They settled on a small studio in Rathmines in south Dublin. 'I believe anybody who has ever lived in Dublin has lived in Rathmines at some point,' says Tibor. 'We had a flat there for six months but you couldn't live there longer because the quality of the studios is so bad. It was safe enough for us but you wouldn't have the kind of security you need when you have kids.'

After three months of searching for work, Aniko secured a position as a carer in a nursing home. 'It was the hardest job I've ever had. Working as a carer is like you're a robot. I had five people to dress and get ready each morning and only had 20 minutes for each of them. Plus I did not understand everything that was going on. At the end of the third week I got a phone call from the Beacon offering me a job in their ICU department. I was so happy.'

Working as a nurse in an Irish hospital was very different to the Hungarian system and it took a while for the couple to settle in. 'The Beacon was a very busy place with high expectations from consultants and colleagues,' says Tibor. 'It was challenging in the beginning.' 'There was a major difference from working as a nurse in Hungary,' adds Aniko. 'Here you have more power and responsibility. In Hungary if you have a problem you go to the doctor because they're always reachable. Here in Ireland, you're the first person patients turn to so you have to deal with many problems alone.'

Tibor and Aniko were also surprised to discover their new colleagues were far more international than the people they'd worked with back in Hungary. 'I remember the first month when I joined the Beacon I saw there were nurses from around the world—India, the Philippines, Australia, the UK, not to mention Ireland obviously—all working with me,' says Tibor. 'In Hungary it's very difficult to see other nationalities because nobody really lives there from abroad. It is quite a strict and closed community. I loved meeting so many different people and hearing stories from their homes and about when they were young. I also liked learning about how they celebrate occasions or how they grieve when they lose someone. They always treated me as an equal. I didn't feel less in any way.

'There was one nurse who was from India and was planning her wedding. It was going to be a huge celebration with 1,500 guests but she hadn't met her future husband yet. I couldn't understand how she was organising her wedding and didn't know the man she would marry. It made me read up about her culture and her traditions. So definitely for us, I feel we've seen a lot more in these eight years here in Ireland than probably we would have ever seen in Hungary because of the nature of our isolated country.'

In April 2010 the couple returned home to get married and a few months later their son David was born. Their second son Akos arrived on the scene in 2013. While Tibor and Aniko had planned to move to a larger home with their children, Dublin's rising rental prices combined with childcare costs meant they had to downsize to a smaller, cheaper apartment near the hospital in Sandyford. Last year the family had to move again but were lucky enough to find a spacious, newly built apartment near the children's school. They had been trying to save for a mortgage but eventually agreed to spend the extra money so they could live in a comfortable apartment close to school and work. 'Having one kid is like a full mortgage and having two of them is like paying two mortgages,' says Tibor. 'To save for a mortgage we could either move out and go somewhere smaller or stay in this safe and spacious apartment. Unfortunately that is the price you have to pay to find a place that is convenient, safe and clean.'

Tibor is happy with the family's home in Sandyford which is located only ten minutes from both the seaside and the mountains. However, he's worried about the insecurity of the rental market and doesn't like knowing that his family may have to move again soon. 'The lack of security in housing here when you don't own your own property is very difficult. I'm really struggling to find a place where I can stay forever providing I'm able to work and pay the mortgage. We have a year's lease on our current home but hopefully it's not going to be the kind of place where they want to rotate people every year. If they came to us at the end of this lease saying we had to leave we would be in massive trouble. It's a very unreliable and harsh environment when you want to find a home. It's like a competition where they line you up and they pick their favourites. The final aim would be to find a permanent home but in order to do that we would need to save a lot.'

In 2016 the family also had to deal with the stress of caring for a sick child. Akos, who was three at the time, had a problem with his throat and needed surgery. The couple decided to return to Hungary for the planned procedure. 'Before Akos got sick I was really keen to go back to Hungary but after that experience I can't imagine being able to work in a hospital there,' says Aniko. 'Basically he was very sick but we were not happy with how the hospital staff handled the situation. The surgeon was fair and did his job but everybody else, I did not like how they reacted. If I said I wasn't happy about something the nurse would start to argue with me. This was not what I wanted when my child was sick.' Tibor says their son's hospital care after his surgery left 'a big scar' on their impression of the Hungarian health system. 'Maybe it was a lack of manpower, maybe it was missing medication or maybe it was just a missing attitude, I don't know. But that situation should not have happened to us. If we had been treated properly with respect and dignity that wouldn't have happened. It wasn't about the procedure, it was about the care that came after.'

Despite the family's unpleasant hospital experience, Aniko still misses home. She also finds it difficult to keep up-to-date with the Irish school system. 'It can be stressful for me. I always feel like everything is new and don't really understand how the education system works here. But what I do like about the schools is that children have more time to learn things. In Hungary children start school at 6 or 7 and have to learn to read and write between September and December of the first year. That is a massive pressure for parents. Here children start earlier and have two years to get the proper reading and writing skills.' Tibor also likes that his two sons are mixing with children from different backgrounds. 'When they go out and play with their school mates one of them is from Saudi, the second is from India and the third is from somewhere else. They see so many faces that I never saw when I was six years old. I believe that is going to help them in the future when dealing with different situations.'

Tibor says the family plans to stay in Ireland at least until the boys finish school. 'My main reason for being here is my kids. I can give them a different future here with more opportunities. For me and my wife we felt we needed to be here, work here and stay here for our sons.' 'The simple thing is the language,' adds Aniko, 'if they speak English they can go to so many countries. Another thing I like about them living here is the positive thinking of the people. Here people take it easy which really helps life. If the kids get into some sort of trouble at school the teachers still highlight the good things and what the children have achieved. That is very different to Hungary.'

The couple speak Hungarian with their children at home in the knowledge that English is their natural tongue with friends. 'David is really bilingual and finds it easy to figure things out,' says Tibor. 'Akos is still a bit small but I see them speaking both languages with no effort.' While Tibor now speaks English with fluency and ease, he still encounters language barriers when communicating in his daily life. 'Anyone who has lived abroad in a different language environment knows that it's not the same. However confident you are, it's not your mother tongue. It's not the way you've expressed yourself for thirty to forty years. Sometimes I still feel that little barrier and have to work on it every minute.'

The couple are eager that their sons maintain a strong connection with their family's heritage and relatives back in Hungary. 'We go there for the holidays every summer and they can do whatever they want there and be completely free,' says Tibor. 'They're so happy to be there and always cry when we leave. We want them to be able to go home and enjoy those days and weeks in Hungary. And if they grow up and graduate and say they want to go back to Hungary, that they've seen enough of Ireland, I would be absolutely fine with that.'

After nearly ten years working in Ireland, Tibor still enjoys his work. He's now a nurse supervisor, a role which involves working with both management and patients on the ward. 'I don't know what it feels like physically to have major surgery but I have seen a lot of people go through that process. So when a patient is vulnerable or in pain and they come to me for help I can tell them that while I don't know exactly how they feel, I have seen many patients in the same situation with similar feelings and can tell them what worked or did not work for them. That is why I'm here; to understand what you are going through and show you a way out of your troubles. It's important for us to be able to listen to patients. Not just because it's our job but because it's important for the patient. We're there to make their lives a tiny bit easier.'

While finding a permanent home has been a taxing ordeal, Tibor says they've made the right decision by staying in Ireland. He is willing to overlook the loneliness he and his wife often feel in order to ensure a happy childhood for their children. 'It's fantastic to live here but it's not always easy. The friends we've made since 2008 are different from friends back home that we'd had for thirty years. Yes, we do have friends here. We have relationships with the neighbours, but it's still lonely. When you have kids your focus shifts towards something completely different from before. I can give them a different future here that is more open to different opportunities. I don't mean they wouldn't have any chances in Hungary but I feel they will have less problems living their lives here. It's challenging to live anywhere in the world with two small kids but I think Ireland gives me more security in my personal life and more opportunities in my professional career.'

2009 Migration

In 2009 the debate around the human cost of climate change began to hit the headlines. While most people were aware of the rise in frequency of storms, droughts and floods across the globe, there was still a real hesitancy to equate these natural disasters with a change in our climate patterns. International Organisation for Migration (IOM) director general William Lacy Swing warned that the consequences of climate change on migration presented humanity with 'an unprecedented challenge'. In 2008 20 million people had been displaced by extreme weather events, compared to the 4.6 million internally displaced by conflict and violence that same year. Lacy Swing estimated that up to 200 million people could be driven from their homes by climate change by 2050.

'Extreme environmental events such as cyclones, hurricanes, tsunamis and tornadoes tend to capture the media headlines, but it is gradual changes in the environment that are likely to have a much greater impact on the movement people in the future,' wrote the IOM director general. 'Climate change is expected to make the world hotter, rainfall more intense, and result in more extreme weather events such as droughts, storms and floods. These changes, in turn, will likely result in further population movements.'[27] In December 2009 world leaders gathered in Copenhagen to discuss the serious challenges posed by climate change. While the 115 leaders acknowledged the scientific case for keeping temperature rises below 2 degrees Celsius, the conference failed to secure a binding commitment on emissions reductions to support the developing countries which would be most affected by climate change.

Meanwhile the effects of the 2008 financial crash and recession that followed continued to impact hugely the lives of migrants with more countries introducing initiatives to persuade immigrants to go home. In Italy the government reached an agreement with Libya which allowed the Italian authorities to return migrants intercepted in the Mediterranean to the war-torn and chaotic North African nation. British Prime Minister Gordon Brown promised to make it harder for illegal workers to enter the country by obtaining student visas and rejected claims that 'portray anyone who has concerns about immigration as a racist'. 'Immigration is not an issue for fringe parties nor a taboo subject,' he said. 'It is a question at the heart of our politics … about the values we hold dear and the responsibilities we expect of those coming into our country.'[28]

In Ireland two budgets were passed during 2009 which saw a reduction in the State's overseas development aid spending and a 15% drop in funds allocated to immigration and asylum services. With unemployment rapidly rising, the Irish Government also introduced changes in June to work permits for immigrant workers. Under the new system, work permits for jobs that paid less than €30,000 per annum would only be granted in exceptional cases while the spouses and dependents of work permit holders could only enter the country to work if they obtained their own permits. Given the continuing economic crisis, and rapidly rising unemployment, it was no surprise that the State was retreating from its once-enthusiastic welcome to foreign workers. Between 2008 and 2009 the number of employment permits issued to foreign workers plummeted by 41%. Asylum applications also dropped 30% to 2,689 in 2009. Overall the number of immigrants arriving in Ireland fell by 26,500 to 57,300 people while the Central Statistics Office recorded a return to net outward migration for the first time since 1995.

Despite the crisis, the Irish people voted overwhelmingly in favour of the Lisbon Treaty after a second referendum was held in October 2009. Taoiseach Brian Cowen hailed the result as proof that Ireland was determined to remain at the centre of Europe. Also in 2009 the Irish Government agreed to accept 78 refugees from the Rohingya Muslim community under a UN-led resettlement programme. The 16 families chosen for re-settlement had been forced from their home country of Myanmar in 1992 following a military crackdown on Muslim minority groups which led to religious persecution, forced labour, rape and torture. Some 250,000 Rohingya crossed the border into Bangladesh in the early 1990s in the hope of finding safety and security and settled in refugee camps.

The French approach to immigrants took an unfavourable turn when the government announced a crackdown on migrants living temporarily in the north-east of the country. The number of asylum seekers camped outside the port city of Calais, hoping to illegally cross the narrow 30km of water to England, was growing rapidly and in September 2009 French president Nicolas Sarkozy ordered the closure of and unofficial camp, known locally as the 'jungle', which had swelled to 1,000 people. The first refugee camp in the area had been opened by the Red Cross in 1999 in Sangatte close to Calais to provide shelter for the mostly Kosovan, Iraqi and Afghan asylum seekers sleeping rough around the city. That camp was closed in 2002 but the new 'jungle' settlement soon followed. Here, hundreds of migrants, the largest numbers from Afghanistan and Pakistan, camped out next to the road where lorries passed en route to the port. News reports in September 2009 described French authorities bulldozing people's make-shift housing while riot officers rounded up nearly 300 mainly young, male asylum seekers.

French immigration minister Eric Besson said clearing the 'jungle' would be an important step in making Calais 'watertight' to illegal migrants. 'There are traffickers who make these poor people pay an extremely high price for a ticket to England,' said Besson. 'This is not a humanitarian camp. It's a base for people traffickers.'[29] Despite these claims, many of the Afghan migrants reportedly gathered under a banner written in Pashto and English which declared: 'The jungle is our house, please don't destroy it—if you do so then where is the place to go?'[30]

A few months previously, the situation of a group of Romanian immigrants living in Northern Ireland was highlighted after more than 100 people, including a five-day-old baby, came under attack in their homes in east Belfast. While nobody was injured in the incident, 20 Romanian families, most of them from the Roma community, had to be moved to a secret location guarded by armed police. 'We are very scared, we have young children,' said one of the victims. 'We cannot go back. Possibly we could go back to Romania but we have no money. We have to stay here.'[31] Deputy First Minister Martin McGuinness described the attacks as 'a totally shameful episode' and called for a collective effort to 'face down these criminals in society who are quite clearly intent on preying on vulnerable women and children.'[32] Writing in *The Guardian*, Fionola Meredith underlined how the attack against the Romanian community demonstrated the two faces of Northern Ireland; the new one where people can work side by side regardless of their background or religious beliefs, and the old, familiar, insular Northern Ireland, 'rooted in tribalism, fiercely territorial, truculent, self-loathing and hostile to outsiders.'[33]

Mohammed Rafique, 2009

Mohammed Rafique's eldest daughter was born on the floor of a makeshift hut in a refugee camp in Bangladesh while torrential rain poured down outside. A few women from the camp had gathered to help Mohammed's wife, Rafika, give birth to her daughter Jamalida. There was no doctor, no nurse and they had no hospital equipment. 'I still remember that morning she was born. We were in a very small hut and there was no electricity. We were so lucky Rafika had a normal birth. Lots of women die with the lack of treatment and no doctors. The Rohingya people had no right to leave the camp for treatment. If you wanted to go to hospital you needed permission. There were women with experience of deliveries who could help but they had no medical experience.'

'After my daughter was born they tried to wash her. They were very scared because so many mothers die during childbirth. Normally when a girl is born the husband is quite shy, it's not like here in Ireland. As this was my first child I was very nervous but when I saw my wife, it's difficult to explain, but I could see through her eyes she was OK. I realised it was a normal delivery and I was very happy.'

Four and half years later, Rafika gave birth to her second daughter Waheeda in a clean hospital bed in St Luke's Hospital in Kilkenny with the guidance and support of a whole medical team—a world away from the dusty streets of her former Bangladeshi home. 'I think it was around 11pm at night and I saw that my wife was going to deliver soon. I rang the ambulance and they came very quickly. The next morning Waheeda was born. There were two nurses and one doctor. There's good healthcare here. I wasn't worried like in the camp. In the camp you were always concerned.'

The Rafique family are part of the Rohingya community that was re-settled in the town of Carlow in 2009. Before arriving in Ireland, Rafique and his family, along with thousands of other Rohingya, had spent nearly two decades living in a refugee camp in Bangladesh. The Rohingya are an ethnic Muslim group based mainly in Myanmar's western Rakhine state, with smaller communities in Bangladesh, Thailand and Malaysia. Often dubbed the most persecuted people in the world, this small Muslim community has endured decades of persecution and human rights abuses. Myanmar's government considers the Rohingya illegal immigrants and treats them as stateless people, denying them citizenship in their homeland. There are severe restrictions on their freedom of movement, access to medical care, education and other basic services.

Mohammed, who goes by his surname Rafique, was 10 years old when in 1992 his parents and seven brothers and sisters were forced to flee their home in Myanmar, formerly known as Burma. A decade earlier Myanmar had enacted a citizenship law stripping the Rohingya community of their citizenship and leaving their people stateless. In 1991 the nation's military regime began implementing the 'clean nation' operation to rid the country of its Muslim minority groups, with widespread forced labour, summary executions, torture and rape. Some 250,000 Rohingya crossed the border into Bangladesh in the hope of finding safety and security.

More than two decades on, the Rohingya's plight continues. In August 2017 violence broke out in the northern Rakhine state when militants attacked government forces. The government responded by killing nearly 7,000 people, including 730 children under the age of five, and forcing more than 645,000 to flee to Bangladesh, a move the United Nations has described as 'ethnic cleansing'. According to medical charity Médecins Sans Frontieres (MSF), nearly 70% of those killed died of gunshot wounds while many others were burned and beaten to death. Rohingya refugees who have made it out of the country speak of massacres in their villages where they say soldiers burned their homes to the ground.

'We had no problem living together with our sister communities and our Buddhist friends,' says Rafique. 'It was a problem created by the military. They were always saying there are lots of Muslim countries in the world and that we must go find our own Muslim country. They wanted a Burma free from Muslims.'

Rafique can still remember the night his family climbed into a boat under the cover of darkness to make the journey into Bangladesh. 'We felt a lot of fear because on one side there was the Burmese military and on the other we were scared of what would happen in Bangladesh. We were travelling with young children and older sick people. We had no food. It was horrible what we went through.' After two days and one night of travel, the family crossed the border into Bangladesh and registered as refugees. They then made their way to the Kutupalong camp where Rafique would spend the next seventeen years of his life. 'In Burma I had no right to freedom of movement and no citizenship. I was born in Burma but they denied us citizenship and said we were illegal immigrants. When we were in Bangladesh they called us Burmese and when we were in Burma they treated us as illegal immigrants. We had history, we had all the evidence that we were born in Burma, but we had nowhere to call home.'

Conditions in the camp were not much better than home. The family lived off rice donations from local NGOs and were denied access to education or freedom of movement. Women and girls feared for their safety in what was often a lawless environment. It was only in 2001 that child refugees were finally allowed access to basic primary education. 'Whatever we suffered in Burma, it was just the same in Bangladesh. The only difference was there was no forced labour in Bangladesh. Some people tried working illegally in the local area but sometimes they wouldn't pay you because you weren't a citizen of Bangladesh. You had no right to a salary.'

Rafique met his wife Rafika while living in the camp. She was just one year old when she left Myanmar and had spent her entire life in the refugee camp. The couple had to request permission from the Bangladeshi authorities before they could get married. Rafique was working as a United Nations Refugee Agency camp community helper when he was selected to be relocated to the UK with his wife. However, he did not want to leave his parents and siblings behind. 'I said I would go anywhere in the world, I have no preference for which country, but you have to let me bring my parents as well.' As the violence in the camp began to escalate, Rafique realised his family were in danger. When he was offered another chance to leave, this time to move to a country called Ireland, he knew it was time to go. 'I explained to my parents and my father said; 'Don't worry about us, go yourself'.'

Before leaving Bangladesh, Rafique and his wife were visited by Irish immigration officials who spoke to the couple about Irish society and culture. They also showed them photos and videos of Carlow town where the Rohingya refugees would live. Rafique remembers watching the opening ceremony of the 2008 Olympics in Beijing, in the camp's community centre, which housed the only television. He waited 45 minutes to catch a glimpse of the athletes from the island he would soon call home. 'I'd never heard that Ireland was a country. We had no chance to read newspapers and had no radio or television. There was no electricity in most of the camp.'

Rafique, his wife and their eight-month-old daughter Jamalida arrived in Ireland in April 2009. They spent their first night in a temporary asylum shelter in Dublin where they were given blankets and food. The following day the Rohingya refugees were brought to the Ballyhaunis direct provision centre in Co Mayo where they spent the next six weeks studying English and preparing for their lives in Ireland. 'It was a big challenge for everyone. We'd never travelled anywhere before. We came here in April and it felt very cold. They organised good quality food for us but we had no language, so we could not ask, 'what kind of food is this?' We were confused and we did not know what was going on.' A total of sixty-four Rohingya people were brought to Carlow in June 2009. 'We came from Ballyhaunis to Carlow on a bus in June, it was summer. We were looking out the windows at the mountains and the forest but we could see no jungle. In Burma if you see forest it's heavy forest. It's jungle.' The refugees were met by men and women from the Carlow Volunteer Centre who had organised a mini-bus to drop them to their homes around the town. A few days later, the volunteers knocked on their doors, ready to show them around Carlow and visit the school, the shopping centre and the GP.

Nearly eight years on, Rafique can call himself an Irishman from Carlow. In 2013 all members of the Rohingya community in Carlow were naturalised and made Irish citizens. For the first time in his life, Rafique became the proud owner of a passport. 'Between 1982 and 2013 I was stateless. I know where I was born but unfortunately I had no right to call Burma my home. I really appreciate what the Irish people have done for us. They gave us the chance to call Carlow home. Now, when people ask where is your home, I can say Carlow is my home town. This citizenship has given me happiness. It has given me a new life, human dignity, the ability to travel and basic human rights.'

Shortly after he received his passport Rafique travelled to Bangladesh to visit his family and see his mother who was quite ill. In early 2017 he returned to the refugee camp, this time with his wife and two daughters. However, when their flight arrived in Bangladesh the immigration officials in Dhaka were unwilling to let his family into the country. 'We had to wait nearly eight hours in the airport and the girls were really hungry. It was very hot, about thirty-five degrees, and Jamalida and Waheeda were really feeling it. I told the officials we had a connecting flight to catch but they treated us like criminals. They said we were not allowed to visit the country. I asked if we could go to a hotel to get some rest and give the girls food. They said we cannot allow you into Bangladesh without permission from a higher authority.' Rafique kept reminding the authorities that he and his family were European passport holders. However, the officials showed no interest in their Irish documents. 'They harassed me and were looking for money as well. I kept saying we have Irish passports and we are citizens of Ireland. I told them we had a return flight, that we had just come to visit my sick parents. I asked: 'Is my crime that I was born into a Rohingya family? Is that a crime?"

Eventually Rafique got in touch with an NGO worker he knew from the Kutupalong camp who went to the airport to vouch for the family and sign a document confirming they would return to Ireland after their trip. Two days later, the family finally arrived at the refugee camp near Cox's Bazaar. They had to apply for permission to enter the camp and were unable to bring smart phones or cameras with them. They also had to return to their hotel at the end of each day as spending the night with family members in the camp was forbidden. For Rafika, it was her first time back in Bangladesh in eight years. 'When she met her mum she was very upset but also so happy. She could not speak for hours after. Everybody was very happy to see the first grandchild and meet the two children.'

Rafique worried that his daughters, who were used to running water and electricity in their Carlow home, would reject his family's lifestyle in the camp. 'Things like going to the toilet were completely different, they had to go outside. But all they asked was if their grandparents were staying in the camp, why couldn't they stay there with them? I was very surprised when my five-year-old girl asked me why some children went to school and others did not. She asked: "Why do some have clothes and shoes and some do not?"' The family spent a month in the Kutupalong camp catching up with old friends and family. 'Being reunited with family and then separated again is not easy. On the one side I was very happy to meet all my friends and neighbours again, but on the other side I was very upset to see their situation. It was very difficult for the girls to leave after meeting their grandparents for the first time. They cried a lot and for two or three days after they got back, they would not calm down. They were very upset.'

Rafique is proud to see his two daughters, now nine and five, thriving in the family's Irish home town. 'I'm really excited to see my girls growing up in Ireland. They have the opportunities now to make friends and go to school. I'm a very proud daddy because their teacher and our neighbours say they are very polite and helpful. We never enjoyed citizenship, but today my girls are Irish and have rights as citizens. My dream is that my daughters can go into higher education and do something for this country. We have been persecuted so much so this is a golden opportunity for our children to go to university. In Burma we had no opportunities.' Nine-year-old Jamalida has recently started asking questions about her family's background and wants to learn more about the Rohingya people. 'Before going to bed she likes to ask about the history of the Rohingya. I tell her a few things that are non-violent. Maybe one day when she needs to write about it for school, then we can share the truth with her. But right now she's too young, I don't like to involve my daughter in those kinds of things.'

Rafique is now an active member of the Carlow Integration Forum and secretary of the Carlow Cricket Club which he helped re-establish in 2011. The club is made up of thirteen different nationalities, with men from Pakistan, India, Bangladesh, Australia, Ireland and New Zealand joining the Rohingya players for training. In August 2017 the Carlow Cricket Club formally reopened with attendance from local TDs and councillors, more than four decades after its closure. The club now has two children's teams— under eleven and under thirteen—a youth development team and two adult teams. They train on the local rugby pitch and recently were offered the use of the sports grounds at Carlow College. 'This year has been a bit of a success for us and we've brought back two trophies and a cup for Carlow. We see that as a good sign for Carlow and that many new members are joining.'

Jamalida trains with the cricket club as well as playing Gaelic football and soccer. 'No matter which sport you play, it's a great way of making new friends and meeting new people,' says Rafique. 'It's a good way of destroying racism. We need to do these positive things for the country. In my opinion, no matter where I come from, I have some responsibility for this country. How can we help with the economic growth and make this country strong? Everybody has responsibilities.' Despite this determination to contribute to the Irish economy, Rafique has been unable to find full-time work in his Irish home. 'A few members of the Rohingya community are working in jobs like security. I do voluntary work but unfortunately I don't drive so it's difficult to get a job here. Finding work is difficult for everyone in Carlow. It's a small town and there are no factories here.'

Watching images online of violence in Myanmar and the recent mass exodus of Rohingya people across the border into Bangladesh has been very difficult for Rafique. He often blogs about his own experiences as a refugee so he can raise awareness of the persecution of the Rohingya people. He hopes one day to study media so that he can add a voice to the international debate about the plight of the Rohingyas. 'Today there is a genocide taking place in my country. Generation after generation of our people have faced these problems. When I was in the refugee camp I never saw news anywhere. Our media was not allowed to speak openly. So when I came here I began blogging and day by day I try to improve my media skills. I spent seventeen years in that camp and my parents have been there for twenty-six years and still the Bangladeshi government does not accept them. They will not even welcome us as visitors. What is the crime of these people? That they're Rohingya? They don't accept us as humankind. I never enjoyed my life in that camp, I never enjoyed my life in Burma, but these past eight years in Ireland have kept me happy. This is my golden life.'

Rafique is particularly grateful to the people of Carlow who he says have provided huge support and guidance in helping the Rohingya settle in Ireland. 'Whenever I meet my friends here they accept me as Irish. We have a good relationship with all the local people. We learn from each other about our languages and societies. Nobody wants to leave their own country, everybody loves their own country. But the people here really welcomed us and understood our feelings. They knew we had been persecuted. When we came here we had no English, but in these eight years we have learned a lot. Without the support of the local people, we never would have settled. In our whole life we were stateless and did not belong to any country. So at least I can now say I have a passport from Ireland. I am from Ireland. I am home.'

2010 Migration

In 2010 Ireland's debate around immigration began to focus on what should happen to young unaccompanied asylum seekers after they turn eighteen. Several charities called for greater support for these youngsters who were being transferred from childcare to a direct provision centre, often in another part of the country. *The Irish Times* reported in May of that year that the Reception and Integration Agency was removing separated children living in Dublin from their schools at eighteen as part of a policy to disperse asylum seekers around the country. 'This can result in the young adults not completing Leaving Cert exams,' wrote Catherine Reilly. 'They are also removed from friends and other support structures they have built up. It could also damage prospects of obtaining leave to remain in the country.'[34]

Barnardos warned that transferring separated children to direct provision centres would only exacerbate 'the vulnerability of these young adults, many of whom have been through long and traumatic journeys and/or have been in care for a long time'. The Irish children's charity called for the introduction of 'appropriate aftercare services' for aged out minors who had either been moved into direct provision or been granted some form of status and left to fend for themselves. 'The majority of these young people come to Ireland at a very young age and become young adults in very challenging and difficult circumstances. They grow up in contrived environments without parents or guardians.'[35]

In its 2010 submission to the UN Committee on the Elimination of all forms of Racial Discrimination, the Irish Human Rights and Equality Commission (IHREC) warned there was 'no consistent or standard approach to the provision of care for separated children.'[36] The IHREC warned of the high incidence of mental health problems among people living in direct provision and the negative impact of not being able to work while awaiting a decision on asylum applications. The human rights group also warned that in the decade leading up to 2010 nearly five hundred foreign children had gone missing from State care and expressed concern that many of these could have ended up as victims of trafficking. It added that most children were going missing when social work supports were limited, particularly on weekends, and called for a guardian or advisor to be appointed to all unaccompanied or separated children.

More generally the arrival of new immigrants into the country fell sharply in the twelve months leading up to April 2010 as the ramifications of the 2008 financial crash continued to affect the country. This also saw the numbers leaving the country soaring, with the Central Statistics Office recording the highest net outward migration since the late 1980s. Emigration rose from 18,400 in April 2009 to 27,700 in 2010, making Ireland the country with the highest net-emigration rate in the European Union. However, the emigration of non-Irish nationals—including Central and Eastern Europeans—fell from 46,800 in April 2009 to 37,600 in April 2010, perhaps indicating a drop in the number of economic migrants unable to find employment Ireland. A total of 1,939 applications for asylum were made in 2010, the lowest since 1996. Nigerians continued to be main nationality to apply for asylum and appeal and there were 6,149 people living in direct provision centres by the end of 2010.

At the other end of Europe, Greece, which had suffered even more catastrophically from the financial crash, was also experiencing a sharp rise in the number of its educated young people moving abroad for work. Meanwhile, the number of refugees arriving on its border with Turkey was steadily rising. Bilateral agreements, including an arrangement between Italy and Libya to support and fund measures to halt illegal immigration across the Mediterranean, coupled with an increased presence of the EU's border agency Frontex on that sea, was pushing asylum seekers further east in their attempts to cross into Europe, resulting in an influx of immigrants on the Greek border.

In October 2010 Frontex declared that Greece now accounted for 90% of illegal border crossings into the European Union. The vast majority of these were taking place at the land border with Turkey, with an estimated 350 people attempting to cross near the Greek city of Orestiada each day. Half of those making the crossing were Albanian workers looking for seasonal jobs in Greece. However the other half was made up of migrants from countries like Afghanistan, Iraq, Pakistan and Somalia who planned to travel through

Greece en route to other EU member states. A total of 53,300 people crossed the Greek-Turkish border in 2010, up from 36,500 the previous year. Of these 2010 crossings, 47,100 were made over the land border and 6,200 by sea. When Greece called for extra support the EU responded by warning that the flow of migrants into the country had reached 'alarming proportion' and activated, for the first time, its Rapid Border Intervention teams, which had been set up to provide additional border guards in cases of 'urgent and exceptional migratory pressure'. Greece also erected a twelve kilometre long fence at Orestiada, forcing immigrants to turn back and consider the option of crossing by boat to the Greek islands.

Across Europe the attitude towards immigration was becoming increasingly negative. The effects of the recession forced many countries, including Ireland, to deepen cuts to integration programmes. The Netherlands' new coalition government—which included Geert Wilders' anti-immigrant Freedom Party—set out plans to slash the nation's integration budget. In France the parliament introduced a ban on face veils in public, a law which the Migrant Policy Institute said intended to show that France would not accept 'a symbol of female oppression'.

Even though by the end of 2010 the number of asylum applications across the EU remained much lower than their peak nearly a decade previously (there were 424,000 applicants in 2001 compared to 259,000 in 2010), the slow but steady flow of arrivals into Greece from the Middle East, Africa and parts of South Asia, such as Pakistan and Bangladesh, continued. Some 55,648 people crossed into Europe that year using the eastern Mediterranean route through Greece. In Italy, these numbers were significantly lower given the recently introduced border control measures, with 4,450 arrivals by water in 2010. Another 6,245 migrants used other routes, such as Spain and Malta, to reach Europe.

As Ivan Krastev would later write in *After Europe* (published in 2017), migration had become the 'new revolution' of the twenty-first century. The Internet had made it possible for young Africans or Afghans to see with the click of a mouse how Europeans live and how their workplaces, schools and hospitals function. 'People rarely compare their lives with the lives of their neighbours anymore; they compare themselves with the most prosperous inhabitants of the planet,' wrote Krastev, adding that democracy in Europe, which had long been an instrument for inclusion, had slowly begun transforming into a tool for exclusion.[37] What was once the European dream of a union without frontiers was in 2010 crumbling into the grim reality of a continent made up of barricades to keep impoverished and desperate foreigners out.

Zeenie Summers, 2010

Zeenie Summers dreamt about her mother the night before she died. In the dream, her mother had been in a road accident but Zeenie was unable to visit her in hospital. She spent the dream walking around the hospital corridors desperately searching for her mother's room but never found it. She woke up the following morning feeling very shaken and immediately told her mother what she had seen. 'There was something so real about it so we prayed together and that helped me feel more relaxed. We used to have this tradition of waking up every morning, sitting in a circle and chatting about our dreams from the night before. My mum was quite superstitious and religious about those things.'

Her mother was getting ready for a cousin's wedding on Lagos Island that afternoon and Zeenie helped by ironing her clothes and packing her bag. Her mother dropped Zeenie's younger brother and sister over to their grandparents' house before catching a ferry to the wedding. 'I think I told her she looked beautiful just before she left. Later that day I was washing clothes in the bathroom when suddenly I went into my bedroom and sat down. The next thing I knew I was standing beside the window crying. I didn't understand what was going on but something in my mind told me my life had just changed and not for the better. I couldn't pinpoint the feeling but the only person on my mind was my mother.'

A short time later Zeenie's aunt called the house and asked that she come join her siblings in her grandparents' house. 'My mum's family is very popular so everyone was out on the street talking and pointing at us. When I got to the house there were loads of people inside. I knew something was up but they wouldn't tell me. I was seventeen at the time and when they see you as a kid they won't tell you anything.' Zeenie eventually found out from her younger sister that there had been a problem with the boat crossing to the wedding. 'When my sister said mummy, uncle and auntie had been in a ferry accident all I could think was 'oh shit, my mum can't swim'.'

She spent the whole afternoon surrounded by family members who refused to reveal what had happened to her mother. Zeenie considered leaving and going straight to the hospital but lost her nerve and stayed in the house. That evening her older cousin took her aside. 'He didn't tell me my mum had died but said I would need to look after my younger siblings now. He told me not to be scared and that this was the time to be strong. When I started crying it wasn't because my mother had died. I cried because I thought to myself I am the first child. Now I am going to have loads of responsibility and have no idea how to deal with it. I was angry rather than sad. It felt like something we could have avoided. I should have known to tell her not to go. My life took a complete turn that day.'

The following morning, shortly before the family's Muslim call to prayer, Zeenie was told the bad news. Her mother had drowned along with nearly forty others in the ferry accident. Her body was brought to the family's home and Zeenie was told to say goodbye. 'They had laid my mum on my bed but there was no privacy for us to be with her. She didn't look dead; she just looked like she had been cleaned. She looked like herself, almost as if she was smiling. When I went into my mum's bedroom my cousins and aunties were going through her stuff and I got really angry. Decisions were already being made for us.'

After the funeral, Zeenie and her siblings were sent to live with their grandmother. They were used to living in an apartment in Lagos with running water and a generator, yet suddenly they were in a different part of the city taking showers in a tiny outdoor cubicle. The family waited to hear from Zeenie's father who had moved to Ireland in 2000. For years Zeenie had been hoping for his return, dreaming of the day her father would come back to his family in Nigeria. She was very close to him before he left and spent a few years as a child living with him in Ghana while her mother stayed in Nigeria with the younger children. He often travelled abroad for work and eventually decided to move to Europe.

'He was only meant to go to Ireland for a year but then one year turned into a decade. We just kept waiting and waiting. He never visited but kept in touch by phone. Every year was a tomorrow that never came. We were waiting for him to come back to Nigeria or we would join him. But my dad liked Ireland too much and decided to start a new life here. My mum assumed I was closer to my dad; that I was his daddy's girl and would always take his side. If ever she was frustrated she would make a passing remark that I kept him on a pedestal and that he could do no wrong. It's true that the only person I was weak for back then was my dad. Whenever I heard his voice I would just melt and do whatever he said. When we asked when are you coming back to us on the phone he always said 'very soon' and we believed him. My mum got mad but I always covered for my dad. She would look at me thinking, 'you don't know anything'.'

As a teenager, Zeenie often clashed with her mother and didn't get on with her cousins. 'They didn't like me because they thought I was proud and I kept to myself too much. Whenever I spoke my mind I got in trouble and I always looked moody. My mum worked as a hairdresser but I was a tomboy and shaved my head. I didn't wear earrings and never wore make-up. She was like, 'what is your problem?'' Zeenie was in her second year of high school when her mother discovered her husband had met another woman in Ireland and they had a child together. 'At that time I was very angry because I thought we were being replaced. After that whenever he called I told my mum to say I wasn't home.'

When Zeenie's father called after the ferry accident to say he had applied to the Irish government for his children to join him in Ireland, Zeenie told him she wasn't leaving. She was studying Literature and Mass Communication at university in Lagos and was not prepared to leave her life and move to a tiny island she knew nothing about. 'I told my dad I didn't want to go to Europe. Because he never came home to Nigeria I had reached the stage where I didn't even believe Ireland existed.'

Zeenie had grown very close to her mother in the months leading up to the accident and was deeply affected by her absence. 'Like depression, people do not really acknowledge loneliness where I am from. It's seen as boredom and expected to pass in a while. So I thought my pain would pass until I realised it had eaten deep into the core of my being.' Even though she was brought up as Muslim, she had also begun reading about different religions as a coping mechanism to deal with her mother's death. 'My family were practising Muslims but I wasn't . One minute I was reading about Buddhism, the next minute I was exploring something else. I didn't believe in the idea of only one god. I had to read everybody's ideas to decide for myself.'

Zeenie's father eventually convinced his daughter to try life in Ireland. The three siblings arrived on Valentine's Day 2010 where they finally met their father's 'other family'. They knew he now had two children with his partner in Ireland but believed he was living separately from them. On arrival, they discovered they would all live in a house together. 'We thought we were his family until we came here and found we were not really that important. I expected to come here and join my father after losing my mum. I was looking forward to feeling secure and being happy again. Coming from the disappointment of my mother's death, my whole life fell upside-down after the move to Galway. I felt so alone.'

Zeenie also discovered that without a Leaving Cert qualification she was unable to study at a university. Her father was eager for his daughter to go back to school, sit her Leaving Cert and study medicine. However, Zeenie made other plans. She moved to Dublin and enrolled in a FETAC

Level 5 journalism course in Dún Laoghaire. Having taken classes in music and theatre in Nigeria, the first thing she did when she arrived in the capital was to look for a choir to join. 'I found the choir in January 2011. If it hadn't been for Discovery Gospel Choir I wouldn't have given Ireland a chance, I would have moved away. But they became my family. I didn't feel so alone and they cared about me and my welfare and even my siblings.'

After an internship with a news publication, Zeenie ended up back in Galway working in the Next clothing store. She tried moving back in with her father and his new family but struggled to adjust. She wanted to go back to Dublin but didn't even have enough money to pay for accommodation in Galway. She ended up registering as homeless with Galway City Council and moved to the YMCA in Dublin. 'I could have gone back home to my father's house but I felt worse than alone there. There was no love for me in his home; no emotional or moral support, no hope and no future. It was toxic so I was better off out of there and on my own. I was in pain because I still had a living parent but felt like an orphan. It was the lowest point in my life. I also thought the only way for me to have a future and a fighting chance for my siblings was to go out on my own, find a way to get future education and secure a job that would help me save money. For some reason the anger I got from my mother's death killed a lot of the fear inside me. I was not scared of offending people or saying what I felt. I wasn't scared to go out and be homeless. I don't think I would have had that courage or strength had I not had the upbringing my mother gave me.'

Zeenie stayed in the YMCA for three months and with the help of a social worker she signed up for welfare benefits and applied for financial support to go back into third level education. She found that her love of sewing and fashion design helped clear her mind. It was around this time that she began to fully acknowledge the fear and loneliness of a world without her mother. 'It was the pain of feeling that nobody was ever gonna watch out for me like my mother did. The thought of not wanting to work towards anything for the future because it wouldn't matter in the end. Because I didn't matter. The thought of her not living in this world again. That was how loneliness felt for me. Even though I had friends and was always involved in many activities and was surrounded by beautiful people, there was still a void in my life they couldn't fill.'

As she gradually settled into life in Ireland, she grew accustomed to the feeling of being different and having black skin in a predominantly white community. 'I didn't know I was black until I came here. I didn't know I was limited, I didn't know people got things according to their colour, it didn't occur to me. The first year in Ireland I didn't consider myself black, I didn't even consider myself Nigerian, I just considered myself Zeenie.' In 2013 Zeenie met her boyfriend David. Building a strong relationship with another person helped her to finally put some roots down in her Irish home. 'It's good to have a best friend in a country that's not your own. Having a person like him makes life much more fun and far more bearable.'

Eight years on from her death, Zeenie is slowly coming to terms with her mother's absence. In August 2017 she made it through the anniversary of the accident for the first time without breaking down into tears. 'Before I would have been so mad and angry. I would have felt a range of emotions like anger, regret, guilt and hate. But now it's become a little more of acceptance. It took me a long time to look at myself and say I am who I am because of my mother. I thought she just brought us up and rubbed off on us but the more I go through life's challenges and think about my life choices, the more I realise how similar we are. That's why I think my mum was the one who influenced me the most. I'm a list maker and I plan, just like her. My dad left everything up to chance and didn't think things through. But you can't leave your life to chance. You can't go to school and just hope for the best. You need to make plans, to be practical and realistic. If I'd listened to my dad and focused on being a doctor I'd be in debt now and probably would not even have graduated from medical school.'

Zeenie is now a singer-songwriter and fashion designer who runs her own online business making custom-made clothes for customers across Ireland. 'I am obsessed with working with my hands and learning all the time. I can't take a break from sewing, pattern drafting and designing for too long. I've sold clothing across Ireland in Limerick, Cork, Galway and the Aran Islands and also in the UK and the Netherlands. I'm not making as much as I would like but it's not as little as I would have feared either. I think if it became too much more I would be overwhelmed.' She has completed a diploma in Business and Law at Rathmines College and gigs with a number of bands around Ireland. She also joined *The Waterboys* as a backing singer on a two-month tour around Europe. 'When I got the request to go on tour the first person I thought to call was my mum. In the past, the realisation that my mum isn't around anymore would be a shock. But it's been eight years now so I'm getting used to it. There are times when I do want to ring her, I still have her phone number in my phone.'

She remains in contact with her father and visits him in Galway occasionally. 'He's older now and you can't keep beating someone for their mistakes. As I've grown up here I've realised he has to live with the consequences of his decisions. I don't need to forgive him and he doesn't owe me anything anymore. So rather than cut him off I show up to visit every once in a while. But we are not close. I think sometimes it's a good thing that the good people die first. Obviously it would have been better if my mother had stayed alive but if she hadn't died, I wouldn't be where I am today. I would have had no reason to come to Ireland and would probably have gone down a different route in life. But everything that has happened in my life has led from that and I'm very thankful for that.' Singing with Discovery Gospel Choir and developing relationships with both Irish and international musicians in Dublin has helped the singer feel at home on this island. 'Music has been the stepping stone to everything else that has opened up for me in my life here. My mum's death led me here and then music helped me to thrive.'

In 2017 Zeenie became an Irish citizen. She was not planning to apply for citizenship but was tired of paying the high cost of visas for trips abroad. However, on the day of the ceremony she was surprised by the happiness she felt. 'The sense of pride on the day was because I'm happy that I'm now a part of Ireland and not a part of Nigeria. Nigeria did not provide anything for me, it was always my mother who provided for me. And when I was bold and tough enough to go out on my own here and fight for something to better myself, the Irish government supported me. They gave me access to education courses. Ireland has done so much more for me than Nigeria.'

'Ireland is also definitely home now. No matter how much I crave going back to Nigeria when I'm feeling down, once I clear my tears I realise I don't really want to go there. I want to go back to the home I used to know when my mum was alive and when there was food or clothes or advice waiting for me. But if I went back now I'd be just as stranded as I was when I first came to Ireland. I am now in a good place and my life picture is much clearer. I have my goals back and they seem achievable. That gives me something to live for.'

2011 Migration

On December 17th 2010 a 26-year-old Tunisian man named Mohamed Bouazizi set himself on fire in protest against the oppression he faced from local authorities. Bouazizi died in hospital less than three weeks later. What followed was a series of mass protests and uprisings known as the Arab Spring, which rapidly spread across the Middle East and pushed authoritarian and dictatorial leaders to end decades of oppression. The movement was initially envisioned as a popular demonstration and social media driven revolution of young Arabs aimed at bringing about peaceful change in their countries. However, it was to result in protracted conflict in Syria and Yemen, the rise of Islamic State as a powerful international terrorist network, the collapse of government in Libya and the mass exodus of millions of people into Europe.

The Arab Spring may have brought about regime change but it did not bring about peace, wrote American diplomat John Price in 2014. 'Without an endgame plan, the changes in these countries only led to chaos. Without leaders who can unify the differing religions, ethnic and cultural factions it will be difficult to ever find peace.'[38] In Syria, this revolutionary fervour kicked off pro-democracy protests in March 2011 in the southern city of Daraa which led to the arrest and torture of a group of teenagers. When security forces opened fire on demonstrators, more people took to the streets demanding the resignation of Syrian president Bashar Al-Assad. By the summer of 2011 government and opposition supporters began to take up arms, leading to violence that would escalate over the following years and result in the deaths of hundreds of thousands of people and the displacement of millions of Syrians.

For Europe, the Arab Spring and government crackdown that followed was to mean one thing above all: the large-scale arrival of migrants. While the vast majority of people who fled Libya and Tunisia in 2011 travelled to neighbouring countries (there was only a small increase that year in the numbers arriving in Italy and Greece), the Arab Spring exposed the 'critical weaknesses and exacerbated long-held disagreements within the European Union related to asylum, immigration and external border control policy matters', according to the Migrant Policy Institute.[39] It began a new debate around the parameters of Schengen cooperation and brought to the surface the question of when and how EU member states might reintroduce border controls. Italy felt that the burden of migrant arrivals should be shared by all EU states and called for greater financial and technical support as numbers arriving from Tunisia and Libya began to grow. However, many member states objected to Italy's proposal to relocate asylum seekers to other countries across Europe.

As revolution and violence spread through the Middle East, much of the EU was still suffering from strict austerity measures in the wake of the global economic crisis. Public resentment of these cutbacks coalesced in many places into a rise in anti-immigrant sentiment and increased popularity for radical-right wing parties. On 22 July 2010, the far-right and anti-Islamic extremist Anders Behring Breivik killed eight people by exploding a bomb in central Oslo. Breivik then opened fire and killed sixty-nine young people taking part in a summer camp for young centre-left political activists on the Norwegian island of Utoya. Meanwhile, in France and Belgium, bans against wearing the Muslim face veil or burqa came into effect and in September, the Swiss Parliament also voted to ban burqas.

In Ireland the Department of Justice, under its newly appointed minister Alan Shatter, published a strategy statement in which they committed to providing 'an immigration system with appropriate policies which meets the needs of a changing society' and which would promote 'equality and integration in Irish society in order to further economic growth, social inclusion and fairness'.[40] Mr Shatter also approved a new pilot project which saw civilian staff from the immigration section of the Department of Justice take up roles as immigration officers at Dublin airport, a duty carried out solely by the gardaí since the 1930s.

Immigration into Ireland increased slightly to 42,300 people in the twelve months leading up to April 2011, compared to 31,000 the previous year. However, according to Economic and Social Research Institute, overall inward migration to Ireland had declined since 2007 with the adult non-Irish population falling to 374,000 or 10% of the population by 2011. The institute explained the small increase in 2011 as returning Irish nationals

Bassam Al-Sabah, Iraq (photo by Dara Mac Dónaill)

Magda Chmura, Poland (photo by Dara Mac Dónaill)

George Labbad, Syria (photo by Cyril Byrne)

Azeez Yusuff, Nigeria (photo by Nick Bradshaw)

Tibor and Aniko Szabo, Hungary (photo by Alan Betson)

The Rafique Family (Mohammed, Rafika Begum, Jamalida, Waheeda), Myanmar (photo by Brenda Fitzsimons)

Zeenie Summers, Nigeria (photo by Sarah Freund)

Carlinhos Cruz, Brazil (photo by Nick Bradshaw)

Chandrika Narayanan-Mohan, India (photo by Alan Betson)

Mabel Chah, Cameroon (photo by James Connolly)

Flavia Camejo, Venezuela (photo by Brenda Fitzsimons)

Ellen Baker and James Sweeney, USA (photo by Dave Meehan)

Maisa Al-Hariri, Syria (photo by Dara Mac Dónaill)

Eve and Maybelle Wallis, UK (photo by Patrick Byrne)

from temporary work-study excursions. Meanwhile, outward migration in 2011 increased sharply to 76,400 departures.

The Department of Justice reported that 83,000 entry visas were processed in 2011. More than 90% of these visas were approved with the vast majority of applicants coming from India, Russia, China, Turkey and Saudi Arabia. Meanwhile, a total of 130,500 non-EEA nationals were given permission to remain in Ireland, with most of these remaining for study or work. The top nationalities that registered to stay in Ireland longer than ninety days were from India, China, Brazil, Nigeria and the Philippines. Some 1,250 people applied for asylum in Ireland in 2011, down from 1,939 the previous year. This number marked a massive drop from the 11,600 people who made asylum applications in 2002 when the system reached its peak. There were around 5,400 people living in direct provision centres by the end of the 2011.

The results of the 2011 census, which was held on 10 April, showed the number of people born overseas living in Ireland had grown from 224,261 people in 2002 to 544,357 in 2011, with a total of 199 different nationalities represented across the country. The number of Poles had risen 94% from 63,276 people in 2006 to 122,585 in 2011, making them the largest group of 'non-Irish nationals' followed by 112,259 UK nationals. The number of Lithuanians, Latvians, Romanians and Brazilians living in Ireland also rose significantly. Galway was named the most multi-cultural city with 19.4% of its residents recorded as non-Irish. According to the census, 514,068 people spoke a language other than Irish or English at home. Among European nationals living in Ireland, Polish was the most common language followed by Lithuanian, Romanian and Latvian.

2011 was also the year the European Court of Justice (ECJ) declared Ireland would have to end its practice of denying the right to reside and work to foreign-born parents of children who were Irish citizens. In response, the Department of Justice introduced a new scheme under which a non-EU parent of an Irish born citizen child could be granted residency on a Stamp 4 basis. Before 2005 all children born in Ireland automatically became Irish citizens regardless of where their parents came from. This arrangement came to an end following the passing of the 2004 citizenship referendum. Since January 2005 all children born to foreign-national parents had to wait to become Irish citizens through naturalisation. Under the new system, one of the child's parents had to be resident in Ireland for three out of the previous four years in order to acquire citizenship for the child.

Carlinhos Cruz, 2011

When Carlinhos Cruz arrived in Ireland he didn't speak a word of English. He had never lived abroad and had spent his entire life under his parents' roof in São Paulo. Unlike his four older sisters who had little interest in travel, he yearned to discover Europe and develop his musical skills overseas. 'Looking back now it seems strange that it didn't faze me more but maybe that's something that comes with age. I didn't care that I wouldn't be able to speak with anyone, I just wanted to explore. The few word of English I did know came from Bob Marley and Nina Simone songs.'

Carlinhos arrived in Ireland with his guitar on his back on his twenty-sixth birthday, ready to begin an English-language course in Dublin. As a young musician growing up in São Paulo, he had always dreamed of living in a European city. He came from a family that had never travelled outside Brazil but met friends at university who shared his passion for adventure. 'Friends are very important. They teach you how to dream and say let's go. I always had more open-minded friends than my sisters. My father had never even left São Paulo and my sisters are in their forties and they belong to a different generation. They had different kinds of friends and didn't dream of travel like me. The image I had in my mind of places like London or Italy was so much better than going to the United States or Australia. I wanted to go to Europe for my music.'

When he finished university, Carlinhos decided to save some money and move to London. He sold his car, quit his job and applied for a visa. His application was rejected and he applied again. On the third refusal a friend suggested he try moving to Ireland. 'I had to come here. I had already stopped my life in Brazil. I had sold everything and had said I was leaving to friends and family. I had to go somewhere. I had liked the idea of London as a big city. I grew up in the suburbs of São Paulo but I loved the city centre: the environment, the craziness, the crowds, the people, the bars. I knew nothing about Ireland but my friend said "Let's go to Dublin. London is very close by so you can visit."

It had taken Carlinhos nearly a year to try and secure a visa for London. It took him less than a fortnight to get an Irish visa. He signed up for a language course in Dublin, booked his flights and flew to Europe. He spent his first few weeks in Dublin living in an apartment on Mary Street with another Brazilian who played gospel music on full volume. 'The first three weeks I always kept my money and my passport in my pocket. I was worried I couldn't trust anyone. But when I heard my flatmate listening to gospel music, I thought he must be OK. He won't steal my money.'

Carlinhos already knew a few Brazilians in Dublin who helped him settle into his new home. He began his English course straight away and spent the first few months rushing from early morning shifts as a kitchen porter to English classes in the afternoon. 'My visa was a year long—six months study and six months holiday. So those first six months I was working as a kitchen porter in a coffee shop. It was very hard to attend my English classes to be honest because I was so tired. I started work at 6am, finished at 1pm and then my classes would run from 1pm-6pm. I always used to fall asleep in class. He was also eager to get involved with the Dublin music scene and started gigging with a Brazilian rock band. After a while he built up the courage to play his own music in venues like Sin É, the Turk's Head and the International Bar. 'Being a musician here opened a lot of doors for me. I made friends with Irish musicians right from the beginning. You start to belong to a group of people that really appreciate your music.'

Moving abroad meant Carlinhos had to learn to survive living independently outside his parents' home for the first time. 'When I realised I had to buy my washing powder and salt for cooking, that was a shock for me. Even toilet paper was like, wow! I'd lived with my parents until I was twenty-six and had never left before.' He says his first few months in Ireland consisted of 'Tesco Value pasta, oversized fleece coats from Penney's and a whole re-education in living'. He discovered that kidney beans from Tesco were a passable replacement for cooking his beloved '*Feijao*' bean stew and met friends who introduced him to 'the laneways and side streets of the city I now call my second home'.

Carlinhos had been living in Ireland for nearly two years when he met Sorcha Ní Mheallláin through a mutual friend. His relationship with the young teacher from Derry introduced Carlinhos to a whole new world of Irish culture and music. 'Before I met Sorcha I'd never been to an Irish marriage or funeral. You're only invited to a wedding or go to a funeral if you've really integrated into society, if you belong and have close friends in a country. Especially Irish weddings and funerals because they're such a big deal here and so completely different from Brazil. It was a really good way to actually feel like I live here. It means that you're a part of Irish life. Sorcha showed me what Ireland really means. She showed me the countryside and brought me to friends' parties. I feel more integrated now because of her and that wouldn't have happened without her. I'm not sure if my experiences would have been better or worse because I was having a very good time before we met but I know so much more now about Irish people.'

While Carlinhos always expressed an interest in visiting new parts of Ireland and meeting new people, Sorcha often worried that being the only foreigner at an Irish gathering would be difficult. 'I didn't find it hard to integrate with his Brazilian friends because I already had a lot of friends who weren't Irish when I met Carlinhos,' she says. 'But I did worry about him at parties with Irish people. I suppose there are a lot of in-jokes here and songs that everybody would know. You don't really encounter that as an Irish person; it's your country and you have the dominant cultural space in some ways.'

Sorcha quickly realised that there were many similarities between Irish and Brazilian culture. 'All the good things I like about Irish culture are definitely present in Brazilian culture and I think music brings that out in Irish people. I would bring my Irish friends to gigs with our Brazilian friends and they would start out like quintessential Irish lads and be really awkward. Everyone would be dancing and they'd be totally out of their comfort zone. But after a few songs they'd suddenly be dancing with everyone. Brazilian music brings out such a nice side of people, particularly the rhythms and the beats. Irish people respond really well to that.' The couple have also found common ground when it comes to their sense of humour. 'Obviously in Ireland we laugh at ourselves a lot and I think that's certainly one mutual point,' says Sorcha. 'If you meet a Brazilian you can slag them or they can slag you and it will go down well. And with that comes the '*craic*' and sense of fun and general positivity.'

While Sorcha was eager to introduce her boyfriend to her Irish friends, it was clear Carlinhos had already fully established himself on the Dublin music scene. 'I'm from the north west of Ireland but I've been in Dublin since university so it's a long time,' says Sorcha. 'Obviously I knew quite a lot of people here and had quite a good social circle. But when I met Carlinhos I just thought, 'I've never seen someone like this'. I called him the Brazilian godfather because at that point he was playing loads of gigs and every Brazilian in Dublin knew who he was. Every Mexican and Venezuelan knew him too. We couldn't walk down the street without a hundred people recognising him.'

When Carlinhos first arrived in Ireland, he sang his music in Portuguese but as time passed and his language skills developed he began writing in English. 'I think more about my music now than before because I can sing in English but also use a real Brazilian melody. I don't have to sing in Portuguese anymore to create the Brazilian rhythms. Portuguese will always be my language but I now feel comfortable enough in English to express myself and be creative. Discovering Irish music and meeting friends who share my love of music from

France, Mexico, Spain and South Korea brought new flavours, textures and ideas to my songs. As long as you are being honest with yourself, there are no limits with music or instruments.'

In 2013, Sorcha moved to Portugal to work as a teacher in an International High School. Carlinhos soon followed and in 2014 the couple moved to Brazil. Carlinhos worked on his music in São Paulo and taught English in a friend's school while Sorcha found work at an international school. However, after seven months in Brazil she decided to move back to Ireland to embark on her postgraduate studies. Carlinhos followed her to Dublin in 2015.

Before meeting Carlinhos and travelling to Brazil, Sorcha already spoke basic Portuguese. However, as the relationship progressed she began to really focus on learning the language fluently. She says being able to speak Portuguese was vital in building a relationship with Carlinhos' family. 'I get on really well with his sisters and I think the fact that I'm very interested in Brazilian culture but mostly the fact that I speak Portuguese has helped a lot. We know quite a few couples, particularly Spanish and Brazilian, and their Irish partners don't speak the language which can be difficult. I think Carlinhos' family really appreciated that I made the effort to speak their language. I can't imagine what my relationship would be like with them if I didn't speak it.'

Back in Ireland, Sorcha's parents had become very fond of their daughter's Brazilian boyfriend. 'I think my parents always saw me as a dreamer but when Carlinhos and I were dating at the start it wasn't serious and I wasn't ready to settle down. I still had flights booked to go abroad and visit other places. So my mum would just tell people that I was 'besotted with a Brazilian'. They were definitely apprehensive at the start but not so much because he was Brazilian, more because he was a musician. But then I brought him home and introduced him and Mum and Dad really started to like him. They saw he was sweet and gentle and someone who would look after me—the things they would look for in a partner.'

The couple make an effort to incorporate Brazilian culture into their daily lives and speak a mix of Portuguese and English at home. 'One of the things I love about Carlinhos is he's so quintessentially Brazilian, which he'll never lose,' says Sorcha. 'He loves Brazil so much and when you see him around Brazilians he just takes on this new identity. We really try to find those elements of the culture he misses and we try to bring it here. That is so important.'

In the summer of 2016, Carlinhos had to make an unexpected trip back home to São Paulo when his eldest sister suddenly became ill. 'She got meningitis with a rare bacteria and died after three days. It was terrible. I went to Brazil and spent two weeks there.' Boarding the plane back to Ireland after the funeral and leaving his grieving family behind was a real challenge. 'It was hard but my life is here. If it wasn't for Sorcha for sure, I would have gone back to Brazil. But at the same time, when a tragedy like that happens it makes you reflect on your own life. I love my parents and my sisters but unfortunately I can't stay there for now. I need to have my own family. That's why I came back.'

Carlinhos now works for an advertising company in Dublin and dedicates his spare time to playing music and finalising material for his first album. 'I like my job a lot but I'm always thinking about my career as a musician and saving money to invest in my new album and pay for new videos. My entire life so far has been working so I can invest in my dream. I hope to take a break for three months, maybe at the end of this year, to finish my album. '

Carlinhos is still close friends with some of the Brazilians he met when he first came to Ireland. While Dublin was expensive when he arrived in 2011, he says the move is far more challenging for Brazilian students arriving in Ireland today. He says most of them find accommodation through Facebook forums before they arrive and often end up being exploited by greedy landlords. 'Renting is really hard in Dublin right now for everyone. But you see apartments with ten Brazilians squeezed in together and it's not about the money. They live together because they can't get references or letters from previous landlords and so they can't rent. When you arrive and only know Brazilian people you'll sleep on their couch. I understand landlords don't like us but something needs to be done. About 80% of the Brazilians who come here are from middle-class or upper-class families because it's not cheap to come here. From our perspective, sending your kids to study English abroad is a big deal. Only 5% of our population can afford it.'

Carlinhos thinks the Irish government should tighten visa regulations for Brazilian students and review the amount of money they need to have in their bank account before coming to Ireland. 'Maybe they could make it harder like in the UK where you need to bring £7,000 (€7,880). Here it was €1,000 when I arrived and now it's €3,000. Maybe they should increase that. We bring money to this country and contribute to the economy. We buy English courses, we buy clothes, we buy food. But I still think something should be done about the visas.'

Sorcha disagrees that raising the amount of money a person is carrying when they arrive in Ireland is the best way of regulating the number of Brazilians moving over. 'I think if it was raised to €7,000 you'd only have a certain type of Brazilian coming here like in London. That would be a shame as it's nice to offer the opportunity for people of different walks of life to come to Ireland.'

The couple are now engaged and have set a date to get married in June 2018. However, they're eager to see more of the world and live abroad again before starting a family together. 'The most important thing for us to remember is to keep ourselves open,' says Carlinhos. 'Even if we never move away from Ireland or if we go to Barcelona next year. It's always exciting to keep those possibilities open. Maybe we'll have our first baby here and go to Brazil for a while and then come back. There are lots of options.' Sorcha agrees that it would be good to spend some more time in Brazil and be closer to Carlinhos' family. 'We're not really sure what will happen but we'd like to be in Brazil again for a bit in the future. We love travelling and living in different places and meeting different people but I don't think we can say anything for definite.'

For now, Carlinhos is happy to continue working on his music in Ireland and says he feels grateful to the country for allowing him to pursue his dreams. 'In São Paulo you always had to prove yourself to your friends and family but here I love it because I can do whatever I want. There is none of the pressure I had there. I can focus more.' Unfortunately if

Carlinhos is serious about progressing his music to the next level professionally, he says he will need to move abroad in the future. 'Dublin is a very small city, especially when you're talking about art. If you really want to dream higher then you have to go to London or America.'

One year on from his sister's death, Carlinhos is still coming to terms with his family's loss. 'It's hard and it's easy being far away. Sometimes I see her photo on Facebook and I forget she's gone because I don't see her every day here. It's such a big thing and I'd like to be there sharing this experience with my family and working through it together. Losing my sister was hard but that's life. I think it's become easier being far away from them because I'm becoming more mature. In the beginning it was very difficult and I sometimes felt I wouldn't make it without them. But I feel more comfortable here now and have built up my strength to stay longer. I love them but I'm thirty-two and it's my turn to live my own life.'

'Ireland is more than just my past and my present, it has become part of my future and I feel so lucky to have something of this wonderful place in my life through Sorcha. I'm really looking forward to hopefully having a family which reflects all the richness of both our cultures.'

2012 Migration

In 2012 the United Nations Refugee Agency (UNHCR) reported that the number of people forcibly displaced by war, violence and persecution worldwide had reached 45.2 million, the highest number in almost two decades, and highlighted the Syrian conflict as 'a major factor in global displacement.' By 2012 the war in Syria had forced 647,000 people to flee their homes to mainly neighbouring countries, marking the largest annual exodus by a single refugee group since 1999 when more than 867,000 people fled Kosovo. In its annual *Global Trends* report, the UNHCR noted that more than half of all refugees worldwide came from five countries affected by war: Afghanistan, Somalia, Iraq, Syria and Sudan.

The *Save the Children* charity warned in November 2012 that 200,000 Syrian refugee children were at serious risk of freezing as winter temperatures set in across the Middle East. While many Syrians had settled in camps in countries like Jordan, Lebanon and Iraq, others were living in makeshift conditions without adequate shelter, bedding or warm clothes in the face of sub-zero winter temperatures. In Lebanon UNHCR reported that 163,000 Syrian refugees had registered or were awaiting registration but that many more had chosen not to register for security reasons. It warned that with latrines flooding, germs roaming freely and the impossibility of maintaining adequate hygiene and sanitation, even those living in the camps were at risk of ill-health and disease.

Further north, Greece announced in December that it had completed the construction of a 10.5km long, 13ft high barbed-wire border fence at the Evros River along the only stretch of dry land connecting the country with Turkey. In 2009 Frontex, the EU border agency, registered 8,800 migrants crossing this land frontier; in 2010 this number rose to 47,100 and in 2011 it reached 55,000. Before 2012, most of the migrants using this crossing were Pakistanis, Afghans, Bangladeshis, Algerians and Congolese, all fleeing instability and conflict in their home countries. Described as 'the main entry point for illegal immigrants from Asia into Europe', the fast-flowing Evros River marking this border ceased to act as an accessible bridge into Europe from the end of 2012.

Anti-immigrant rhetoric in Greece—a nation crippled by unemployment, wage cuts and harsh austerity measures—began to spread rapidly after the far-right party Golden Dawn secured 18 out of the Greek parliament's 300 seats in 2012. Campaigning under the motto 'Get the stench out of Greece', Golden Dawn were accused of acts of violence against immigrants including stabbings, beatings, and attacks on immigrant-owned shops. The group, described by the UK *Daily Mail* as 'a neo-Nazi party who advocate forcing immigrants into work camps and planting landmines along the border', also set up its own 'pure' blood bank, providing and accepting donations to and from Greeks only.[41] The party also offered help to landlords seeking to evict immigrant tenants.

While there was no equivalent to Golden Dawn in Ireland, the Economic and Social Research Institute (ESRI) did report a fall in 2012 in Irish people's openness to immigration and willingness to accept immigrants into the country. It noted that in 2002 just 6% of Irish nationals had said no immigrants from poor non-EU countries should be allowed entry, while by 2010 22% of people said no immigrants at all should be allowed into Ireland. The report's author, Dr Frances McGinnity, wrote that the rapid growth in the immigrant population, followed by economic recession, had resulted in 'increased concerns about, and resistance to, immigrants in Ireland'.[42]

The ESRI's research coincided with the release of the 2011 census results, which showed the number of foreigners living in Ireland had increased from 224,261 in 2002 to 544,357 in 2011, or 12% of the total population. The number of Poles living here had increased by more than 90% between 2006 and 2011. Indians were the largest non-EU nationality at work in Ireland with a total of 16,986 living in Ireland, up from 8,460 in 2006. In contrast to this dramatic increase in foreign-born people resident in Ireland, there was a continued decrease in the number of applications for asylum: there were just 956 applications in 2012, down by a quarter on the previous year. By the end of the year, 4,841 people were living in direct provision accommodation, a decrease of 11% on 2011. In 2012 the average length of stay in a direct provision hostel was nearly four years, with 59.3% of people spending more than three years in the system. Nearly 10% of residents had spent more than seven years in the system.

A 2012 report from the Dublin-based Integration Centre, called for Ireland to approach the increase of immigrant workers as 'an opportunity to be embraced rather than a cost to be minimised'. The report, which examined the economic and business implications of migration, stated that before the financial crash, immigration had been seen as 'a major opportunity' for the Irish economy and that it was 'crucial not to lose the potential of migrants' living in Ireland. 'Immigration is generally a win-win situation, but for some in society that is not a message that they want to hear. Those in rich countries tend to over-estimate the costs of immigration and under-estimate the benefits. A better-informed debate on immigration is essential in every country, but particularly in a country like Ireland that historically has seen significant levels of outward migration, and in more recent times, significant levels of inward migration ... For economic, business and social reasons it is essential that every possible effort be made to fully integrate immigrants as quickly as possible.'[43]

Chandrika Narayanan-Mohan, 2012

When Chandrika Narayanan-Mohan reflects on the years she spent growing up in India it often feels like a dream. Life in the Rashtrapati Bhavan Indian presidential residence—with its three hundred rooms, sprawling gardens, badminton courts and swimming pool—seemed normal at the time. 'I did things like cycle around the palace gardens and rollerblade around banquet halls. We had a cinema in the house and I had a giant birthday party every year with a ferris wheel and fairground rides.' Two decades on, sitting in her tiny studio apartment in Dublin, the granddaughter of the former president of India reiterates how much life has changed since those years in New Delhi. 'Looking back, it just feels like someone else's life. It was a completely different time.'

Chandrika's grandfather, KR Narayanan, was elected president of India when she was nine years old. Despite living in the presidential palace, she says her family were 'bizarrely grounded'. Growing up as an only child surrounded by bodyguards, maids and drivers, she's still surprised she turned into such a normal adult. 'I could have been the worst human being ever. But my family were low-key as people. Somehow we never felt like an abnormal family.' She remembers her mother always expressing excitement and interest in the ornate furniture and artwork dotted around the presidential estate. 'My grandfather, her dad, had been an ambassador as well so she had the same upbringing as me and lived in nice houses. But she always got excited about things that were new or fancy and that was infectious. It meant I never took for granted the beautiful things around me.'

Chandrika was born in India but when she was three years old she moved to Washington DC with her parents – her mother was a diplomat and her father worked for the World Bank. She remembers their house was in a small suburban neighbourhood where children played on the streets after school. After three years in the United States, Chandrika and her mother moved back to India to live with her grandparents. 'India was a totally different kind of life. We were suddenly in a city where you can't really walk around. It was pretty overwhelming living in a palace with these huge historical gardens.' After six years in India, when Chandrika was thirteen, her mother was posted to Sweden and they moved to Stockholm. Suddenly the young teenager was able to move around a city without a bodyguard following on her heels. 'It was amazing to move to a city where I could walk. I thought the transition would be hard but found I was far happier and more comfortable living in an apartment. I went from travelling with an armoured jeep with six guards carrying machine guns to being able to walk to school through snow in the morning. I felt like a real person again.'

At sixteen, Chandrika and her mother moved to Turkey, the country she still considers home. 'I thought to myself I have a clean slate here and I have one and a half years of school left. I have to make friends quickly and efficiently.' Fortunately, her Turkish classmates were very open to the new arrival from Stockholm. 'My first day of school was four days before my seventeenth birthday so I fully expected to just go home and have dinner with my mum. In Stockholm it had taken time to make friends because when you're the new kid people think you're weird. But in Turkey it was totally different, everyone wanted to talk to me. They were so friendly and on my birthday they took me to this café and taught me how to smoke shisha.

Chandrika did not speak Turkish and often struggled to keep up with gossip and jokes in the language. Fortunately all the students at the school spoke excellent English. 'They were awesome people, very intellectual and fun. When I left Sweden everyone had discovered binge drinking there and it wasn't for me at the time. But when I moved to Turkey you went for a beer or a wine but you also drink tea. It wasn't too boring or wholesome; the café culture just suited me better. You had sixteen-year-olds talking about books and history and that's how I learned about philosophy and Pink Floyd. For me Turkey's still very much home.'

When the time came for university, Chandrika decided to study art history and English literature in York. 'When you've grown up going to international schools your options for university are really Britain, Canada and America. My family was always very literary. We'd read poems and books and I was interested in English literature. We did a trip around England so I could get an idea of the campuses and I fell in love with York. It was so beautiful. I printed out photographs of the city and pasted them in front of my desk to make sure I studied enough to go there.' In York Chandrika met the people she calls her 'chosen family'. As international students the group of friends rarely saw family during term so relied on each other as they navigated through their first years of independence away from home. 'The nice thing about universities in the UK is they breed those relationships because people only go home every few months. You're chucked into this campus life and forced to grow up very quickly. You have to learn how to compromise and do all those things I wasn't used to. I find people in Ireland don't always develop those relationships at university because they don't experience that same cabin fever. It seems like everyone in Ireland has their own families to go back to at the weekend.'

After college the group of university friends moved to London together where Chandrika studied for an MA in art history. After graduating she secured three internships; an unpaid position with the Victoria and Albert Museum, a paid graduate internship at Christie's auction house and a third internship with a gallery that would become her first job. 'I'm fully aware of how privileged I am that my parents could support me during those internships. Most people can't do that.' Despite working in some of the world's top art institutions, Chandrika never felt comfortable living in London. 'It was just really big and I felt dwarfed by everything. London was like an abusive relationship. You grow to love it but it beats you down.' She was forced to abandon plans to do a second master's in arts management when a change in UK immigration rules meant she had to leave the country. 'I had a letter from the university saying, 'We want to accept you but are forced to reject you.' That was a huge shock. All of a sudden I had two weeks to figure out a new country to go to.'

She began searching online for master's courses in arts management and came across an Irish university she had never heard about. 'I thought UCD was some made-up polytechnic. I knew about Trinity and literally nothing else.' She applied for the course and was relieved when a week later she was given a phone interview and was accepted into UCD. By the end of August 2012 she was living in Dublin.

Chandrika met Irish and foreign students in her class at UCD but struggled to build friendships like the relationships she'd left behind in London and Turkey. 'Ireland is a very small place, and people have their own friends from school so they hang out with the same people. When we were on the course we were very close but after we split up they went back to their Irish friends or left the country.' Chandrika spent her free time during those first few months in Dublin exploring the city alone and going to literary events and theatre. 'It was completely new for me. I only had a vague interest in theatre but when I saw the plays going on in Dublin, I thought they were incredible. Dublin was small but electric. There was so much to encourage and support you as a writer or performer here. Dublin provides a stage for people.'

After graduating from UCD, Chandrika worked at Business to Arts and the Irish Architecture Foundation. She subsequently secured a position as the Arts and Culture Manager at the Liquor Rooms bar in Dublin where she found a new group of friends. 'I loved the team I worked with in the Liquor Rooms, they were great people and kept me really sane. I got to meet loads of people from different communities who I would not otherwise have met.' However, even with these new bonds, she struggled to ignore the feelings of loneliness and despair that had begun to plague her mind. She later realised that her complete reliance on friends to stay positive was neither a healthy nor a sustainable way to live, particularly with so many people coming and going in Dublin. 'My real trigger for depression is incredible loneliness. We can all end up lonely because we don't find the people who understand us and when we do find them they're foreign and they leave or even when they're Irish they often leave too. Every best friend I've had since I moved here has left so that's why I gave up on trying to make friends. I couldn't take that level of disappointment anymore.'

Two years ago, Chandrika began attending psychotherapy sessions to try and make sense of what felt like a dark cloud hanging over her life. 'It made me angry that I was living through a WhatsApp group with friends who were abroad. I think ploughing through with that therapy and tearing apart why I was so desperate for friendships made me realise that I needed to accept my friends were far away from me. It was really hard but I had to remind myself that even though they're in America, Brazil, Turkey and Mexico, they're still just a text away.'

Unfortunately, Chandrika's struggles with her mental health coincided with a roadblock in the renewal of her visa to stay in Ireland. In early 2017 her employment situation changed meaning that Chandrika needed to renounce her previous work permit and reapply for a new one under a different employer to continue her job at the Liquor Rooms. There was no guarantee that this permit would be granted. Meanwhile, Chandrika had already begun researching job opportunities with charities and arts groups around Dublin and in March 2017 she was offered a position as marketing and fundraising executive with Fishamble Theatre Company. Aware of the long and arduous process of applying for visas, Chandrika immediately began preparing her application for a new work permit and in April she submitted the relevant documentation.

She knew the response could take months but was confident her application would be accepted. 'To apply for a work permit you have to mail in your old permit so you're stuck in limbo and can't work. I would describe it as jumping off a ledge onto another ledge but you don't know if there's even a ledge there. That's what my life was like as an immigrant; jumping and just hoping for the best.'

The Department of Business, Enterprise and Innovation website indicated that Chandrika should expect to wait two months for a response to her application. Her initial plan was to spend time with her mother in Switzerland and her father in India while she waited for an answer but her lawyer quickly explained she should not leave the country until her visa was confirmed. She was also not legally permitted to work. 'It felt like someone asking me 'would you like to have some hardcore depression? There you go.' I had been overworked for years so I decided I had to sit on the sofa and force myself to feel relaxed. I tried to enjoy it and told myself I could wake up late, read books and actually enjoy my life. But I had this awful anxiety building up inside me. I felt so trapped. I couldn't work but still had to pay rent and was stuck in a house I didn't really want to live in anymore. It's hard to feel like you own your life when everything is in the hands of a civil servant.'

With no job, no certainty and no sense of purpose to her life, Chandrika fell deeper into depression as the weeks passed. 'It was awful. Basically I decided two months into it that if it got rejected I would consider killing myself. It was totally irrational, it's not even that the situation was that bad. But I had really bad depression and horrible anxiety. I'd been given zero security in my life and I didn't feel at home in the

house I was living in. It was a bad mix of everything.' Every
few days, Chandrika would log onto the Government's online
visa system to check on the status of her application. On 14
June, she signed in as usual only to discover the words 'status
refused' beside her name. Rather than fall completely to pieces,
Chandrika's response was to call her lawyer who immediately
began preparing the appeal. She also had the support of the
team at Fishamble. 'I had been a giant blob for three months
and within an hour of my visa being rejected I had found a work
table at the Fumbally Exchange (not-for-profit co-working
space) and had signed up for volunteering. I just geared back
up and decided, let's do this.'

The waiting process for the visa appeal was a completely
different experience to the previous few months. 'I suddenly had
somewhere to go everyday when I got up in the morning. I had
a community who understood me at the Fumbally Exchange
and was surrounded by multidisciplinary and creative people
who were funny and kind. It felt like these were the friends I'd
been looking for for five years.'

Chandrika continued seeing her therapist on a weekly basis.
'She told me, 'you've spent months imagining the worst but now
the worst has happened so how do you feel?" I felt like it was
going to be OK. I didn't want to end my life, I wanted to get
things done. It totally lit a fire under me.' She also kept busy
by sending emails about her visa appeal to local representatives.
She expected to have to wait another five months for an answer
but in August she learned her appeal had been accepted. She
was finally able to begin her new job with Fishamble, who had
kindly waited since March for her visa to come through, and
soon afterwards moved into a studio apartment in the city centre.

'Suddenly I had the job I'd always wanted and was working with the kindest and most competent people I had ever met. The Fishamble team are not human, they're like angels.'

Chandrika recognises how fortunate she was to have help from her father to pay the rent while she waited for her visa. 'He supported me which is not something you want when you're twenty-nine. But I had no other option; you're not allowed to work, you're not allowed to go stay with parents but you have to pay rent. I imagine everyone else in my position just packs up and goes home.'

Chandrika says speaking openly about her struggle with depression, both in therapy and more recently with friends, had helped her develop a new appreciation for her own—somewhat less conventional—family. 'Being an only child and always moving around I never had a home. My dad and his brother live in homes that they own but my mum, her sister and I rent places and I keep my stuff in storage. But as you get older you realise that you don't need the perfect nuclear family. It's almost like beforehand my brain was dismissive of my family because it wasn't the fantasy family I wanted. But I do now appreciate that I have an actual family. It's almost like I had forgotten I had them.'

After five years in Dublin, Chandrika finally feels she's building long-lasting friendships. 'I guess I do now have people who I can call over and chat to. That would have been inconceivable to me, even earlier this year. If someone had told me you're going to be living in your own place where you can welcome people and you'll have at least ten people you can text to hang out with, I would have said that's impossible.'

For now, Dublin is home. However, Chandrika continues to struggle with her sense of identity. Even though she carries an Indian passport, she doesn't feel strongly connected to her parents' home country, particularly because English is her first language. 'My grandmother was Burmese, my grandad was Indian, and they spoke English together. So my whole family on my mum's side spoke English as our first language. I wish I had been brought up with Hindi as a first language because I still don't have a very good grasp of it. I haven't spoken it in years. It's hard to be Indian and not know the language fluently.' She identifies as a 'third-culture kid': a child raised outside their parents' home culture. 'When I learned about third-culture kids, it was like I'd found my nationality. They have a different sense of national identity. When you ask where's home, they either don't know or have a few different places.'

Now that her work visa is secure for another two years, Chandrika is finally planning a visit to her mother in Switzerland over Christmas. 'When I worked in the drinks industry Christmas was our busiest time of year, there was no way you could leave for two weeks. But now me, my aunt and my mum are going to have Christmas together for the first time in four years.' She is also determined to take care of her mental health and prevent her mind from falling back into depression. 'The past year has been insanely overwhelming but it almost feels like I can't complain because all these good things have happened. It's just going to take a good while to recover from many years of depression and anxiety. On paper everything looks amazing but things are not wonderful yet. Therapy is helping to pick things apart and slow down my brain. I'm still exhausted but I'm happy.'

2013 Migration

'I had never seen so many people in the water. Their limbs were thrashing, hands grasping, fists punching, black faces flashing over then under the waves. Gasping, yelling, choking, screaming. Oh God, the screaming! The pitch of it! The sea boiling and writhing around them as they kicked and lashed out, clinging to each other, grabbing at pieces of driftwood, snatching handfuls of water as they tried to clutch at the top of the breakers. They were in a frenzy of desperation, shrieking at us, trying to attract our attention on the little boat.

'I never wanted to tell you this story. I promised myself I would never tell this story again because it's not a fairy tale ... Do you understand what I'm trying to say to you? Maybe it's not possible for you to understand because you weren't in that boat. But I was there and I saw them. I still see them. Because it's still happening.'[44]

On 3 October 2013 an overcrowded trawler filled with migrants from African countries fleeing war and poverty sank near the Italian island of Lampedusa. Some 366 people, most of them from Eritrea, died that day in water only 800 metres from the Italian shore. BBC journalist Emma Jane Kirby, who wrote the story of Carmine Menna (see above)—the optician who with a group of friends on a yacht saved forty-seven people that day—warned that reports of migrants arriving in Europe had become so commonplace that it was 'almost becoming meaningless'. Pope Francis described the deaths as 'a disgrace', while Italian deputy prime minister Angelino Alfano called on European leaders to remember that 'this is not an Italian but a European disaster'.

'A terrible human tragedy is taking place at the gates of Europe and not for the first time,' said Jean-Claude Mignon, head of the Council of Europe's parliamentary assembly. 'We must end this now. I hope this will be the last time we see a tragedy of this kind, and I make a fervent appeal for specific, urgent action by member states to end this shame.'[45]

The Lampedusa tragedy led to renewed political discussions around how to deal with the numbers of migrants arriving in Europe and how to relieve the burden from southern countries like Italy and Greece. Italy's response to the deaths was to launch the *Mare Nostrum* naval operation to tackle the humanitarian emergency in the strait of Sicily between Italy and Tunisia. Meanwhile, the European Commission reassured ship captains that helping migrants in distress would not lead to sanctions and that 'they would not face any negative legal consequences for providing such assistance'.[46] The Commission also urged all European countries to get involved with resettlement and open their doors to asylum seekers, saying it intended to make a lump sum of up to €6,000 available per resettled refugee.

Meanwhile the conflict in Syria continued to escalate, with hundreds of people killed in August after chemical weapons were fired at several suburbs of Damascus. United States president Barack Obama responded to the Assad regime's attack by ordering a targeted military strike in Syria. Obama described the images of men, women and children lying in rows, killed by poison gas, as 'sickening'. 'On that terrible night, the world saw in gruesome detail the terrible nature of chemical weapons, and why the overwhelming majority of humanity has declared them off-limits—a crime against humanity, and a violation of the laws of war,' said Obama. 'Our ideals and principles, as well as our national security, are at stake in Syria, along with our leadership of a world where we seek to ensure that the worst weapons will never be used.'[47]

The United Nations Refugee Agency had already announced in June that it was looking for 10,000 places for humanitarian admission of refugees from various countries and 2,000 places for the resettlement of Syrians in acute need. A number of countries stepped forward to offer assistance including Germany and Austria who committed to accepting 5,000 people each. By the end of 2013 Lebanon, a country of four million people, was hosting more than 880,000 Syrian refugees. In Jordan the Za'atari refugee camp in the north of the country initiated plans to turn the camp of more than 120,000 people into in a temporary city. With most Syrian refugees still fleeing into neighbouring countries, the vast majority of migrants crossing the Mediterranean were still coming from Sub-Saharan countries in Africa, particularly Somalia and Eritrea. In the first six months of 2013, an estimated 8,400 asylum seekers had already landed on southern European coasts, mostly in Italy.

Meanwhile, Europe experienced a growth in the movement of economic migrants after Croatia joined the European Union in 2013, with Croatian citizens now free to work in most EU countries without restrictions. While many celebrated the end of another European land border, the debate around 'welfare tourism'—EU citizens taking advantage of welfare benefits in member states outside their home country—was gaining momentum. European Commission vice-president Viviane Reding rejected the growing perception that people walking down high streets with foreign accents were 'welfare tourists' and reasserted her support for protecting the freedom of movement for EU citizens across the union. 'Who are mobile EU citizens?' she asked in October. 'The vast majority of these persons move to work ... They are more likely to be of working age, more likely to be economically active and more likely to be in employment than nationals. This means that they contribute their share to national security schemes ... The share of those who are economically inactive is small.'

In Ireland immigration continued to fall, with data showing that the overall numbers of immigrants decreased by more than 50% between 2008 and 2013. Arrivals from the EU accession states of Central and Eastern Europe fell most significantly during this period, dropping by nearly 80%. By the end of 2013 about 120,000 non-EEA nationals had received permission to remain in Ireland, the majority of whom had come to the Republic for work or study. Most of these visa holders came from India, Brazil and China. Meanwhile emigration continued to rise with a total of 89,000 people leaving the country in the 12 months leading to April 2013 (of these, 59,000 were Irish citizens). The decline in applications for asylum continued through 2013 with just 946 applications received by year's end. The largest number of applications came from Nigerian nationals followed by applicants from Pakistan, the Democratic Republic of Congo, Zimbabwe and Malawi. By the end of 2013 there were 4,360 people living in direct provision centres.

The enactment of the Criminal Law (Human Trafficking) Amendment Act in 2013 led to a debate around human trafficking, particularly among women and children who were at particular risk of sexual exploitation. The Council of Europe reported in September that Ireland needed to improve its method of identifying human trafficking victims and warned that the number of prosecutions and convictions for trafficking in the State remained very low. While the report recognised the adoption of the new human trafficking act, it called on Irish authorities to give NGOs and other members of civil society a formal role in identifying trafficking victims, which would separate the process from police investigations and criminal proceedings. By the end of 2013, 44 victims of human trafficking had been reported to or detected by gardaí. Of these, more than a third were children while the majority were female.

Mabel Chah, 2013

Mabel Chah's parents were never happy with their daughter's decision to become a professional singer. They knew she was talented but felt they needed to be realistic about the opportunities available to a female singer from Cameroon. 'My mother always had her doubts and would tell me I was born in the wrong part of the world. She said I could be passionate about music but that was it. My father would have none of it. No parent will accept their child dropping out of school to become a musician. But I didn't care because I really loved singing. Initially the support from my family was nil but after the first stages of the competition they saw my ambition was actually starting to become something.'

Mabel was in second year of university studying translation and interpretation when she dropped out to pursue a career in music. Soon after she discovered the internationally recognised Nestlé African Revelation singing competition was coming to her region to hold auditions. Growing up in an English-speaking province in south-western Cameroon, Mabel was used to being ignored when it came to music events and competitions in a country where the majority of people speak French. She lived in a society where, as an English speaker, she often felt marginalised and forgotten by her nation's decision makers. But for the first time, the Nestlé competition was inviting English-speaking musicians to take part and Mabel quickly convinced a group of friends to join her in trying out.

The four-piece band successfully made it through the regional stage of the competition and was invited to take part in the national finals. 'The finals were held in a French speaking province and the votes depended on the reaction of the public and the judges. We had just two people in the audience supporting us. We went on stage and stood in front of about fifteen hundred people and there were only two voices screaming support for us.' The group, which was called Baam, had composed a song in three languages—English, French and Pidgin English—a move that helped them stand out among the other competitors. 'Maybe it was the harmonies or the chemistry but by the time we were done singing the first chorus the whole crowd was cheering. Considering where we came from that felt amazing. We were singing in three languages and that was the advantage we had over the other groups who sang only in French.'

The band ended up winning the Cameroonian leg of the competition and was invited to take part in the international competition in the Ivory Coast in 2008. 'We competed with all the African countries and when the results came in we discovered we'd won. It was such a great feeling. We signed a deal and recorded our first single in Paris. Then we went back home and recorded the album.' As the winners of the Nestlé competition, the group was automatically assigned a manager. However, the man chosen for the job was a French speaking Cameroonian. 'He had no idea what to do with our work.

It was the first time an English-speaking band had reached that musical level in the country. I still say if he had put a real effort into us, considering what's happening with that type of music in Cameroon now, we would have gone places as a group because our songs were very rich. We were great singers, all of us. But he was more used to working with French artists and they have their own kind of music. So the project just died out. 'We stayed together right up until around 2011 but we struggled to do it on our own and the group fell apart. We organised some performances but how much could we do? With only 20% of the country speaking English, that kind of music was still not understood.'

Six years on, Mabel says the group is still highly regarded in the English speaking regions of Cameroon. 'Even now people say well done. Many artists will thank us and say you showed us what was possible and opened the door for a lot of us. Back then nobody would listen to youthful English-speaking music in Cameroon. But today it's the only thing being played on their radios. It shows people that against all the odds, you can do it.'

As she grew older, Mabel found it increasingly difficult to accept the divides that existed between English and French speakers in her country. 'I think the problem is that the government is dominated and ruled by the French speakers. There are many French speakers in the country who don't have it easy either but the government and rules and legislation always favour French-speaking Cameroonians. If you want to get a prominent job you need to be a French speaker. It's very frustrating for English speakers, there's just a level they cannot reach.' Mabel also found being an English-speaking woman in Cameroon made life even more complicated. 'I'm a female from a minority part of Cameroon so you are not taken seriously with all types of opportunities. No matter how much people argue that there is gender equality in Africa, a woman cannot earn the same as a man. Priorities are given to men. Maybe someday we will get some kind of gender equality but I don't think it will happen in my lifetime.'

After Mabel's music group fell apart she found a job with a communications agency working with a chain of restaurants and hotels. She also became more vocal about the unfolding crisis and unrest in the Anglophone regions of her country and called for English-speaking Cameroonians to stand up for their rights. 'When you become too opinionated or vocal, it makes people uncomfortable. It was to do with the political situation in my country. I was tired of people folding their hands and saying "we're not doing anything." There were no women talking for the cause of the English speaking Cameroonians or the causes of the masses. Very few women would dare to venture into that area even today. I don't know what I was thinking; I don't know what got into me. But I thought I could say something about the situation and get away with it. But it didn't go well.'

Mabel began receiving threats after speaking out about the political situation but didn't let the negative response worry her. However, things changed when people turned on her family. 'I really did not care when it was just me but if your family is threatened because of you, if they're not coming for you but for your loved ones, something has to change. I needed a place where I could be safe and if I had something to say I would get help as opposed to being shut down. I was advised by friends to leave. They said if you speak that way you will have to go. These were people who knew what they were talking about.'

With the support of a network of friends and contacts, Mabel made it out of the country and arrived in Ireland in August 2013. She recalls the shock of hearing an announcement being made over the loudspeaker in Dublin airport and not understanding a word. She had been told by the people who arranged her passage abroad that she was going to the UK and had presumed Ireland was a region of Britain. 'I'll never forget the way I felt in that moment. I panicked. Where was I and what language did they speak here? I thought I was going to the UK where they spoke English. The Irish language hit me in the face.'

She declared herself as an asylum seeker in Dublin and was brought to the Balseskin direct provision centre in Finglas, a place where most people seeking asylum spend their initial weeks in the country. She immediately felt isolated and lonely in the hostel on the outskirts of Dublin. 'I knew nothing about asylum or seeking asylum before coming here. The person helping me to leave Cameroon told me to seek protection because I couldn't afford to live here by myself. The centre felt distant because you're made to know it's just a transition reception centre before you're sent somewhere else. It's in the middle of nowhere; it's like you're frozen out. You don't know if you'll be there a month or longer so you can't make plans. You're put into a room with two other women. You've got a Christian sharing a room with a Muslim and that causes conflict for prayer hours. There were so many problems, I needed to get out of there.'

'I came from a city called Douala, with millions of people, to a place in the middle of nowhere. Not seeing people or anything happening around me was too much, it was too sudden. I only spent a month in Balseskin but you see some people staying there for five years and I don't know how they do it. You see the person they were and who they become after five years there. Your ideas change, your dreams change. I didn't want any of that.'

Mabel was moved to the Globe House direct provision centre in Sligo town and immediately began contacting choirs and community groups to find activities to keep her occupied. 'The only time I would go back to the hostel was to lay my head down and sleep. I was thinking if I'm ever going to settle into this community, then I have to make it work for myself.' She felt much more comfortable living in a town on the west coast of Ireland than in an isolated suburb on the outskirts of the capital. 'From the day I entered Sligo I loved the place. It was the fresh air and the fact that when I got off the bus I could see people and houses around me. Everything was close by. My impression of living in Dublin was always a sense of distance.'

Eager to continue making music, she joined the Sligo cathedral choir and the Sligo Gospel Choir. 'I went to the reception in the centre and asked what activities were happening in Sligo and said I love to sing. From there I was directed to different choirs. The Sligo gospel choir was the first family I had here. It was so multicultural with people from everywhere—Asia, America, Africa and Europe.' She also joined the town's cathedral choir where she met Irish people from the surrounding area. 'I stepped into that choir and I was the only African to sing with them. Even now, I'm still the only African singer. Most of us who come from Africa and other war torn areas, when we arrive we think everybody's life here is milk and honey. But unless you go out and not only tell your own story but also listen to other people's stories, you'll never understand that life is not easy for anybody. Not even the people in the choir were having it easy.'

Mabel was invited to join Sabona Community Productions, a group formed by people living in direct provision with the support of local actors and writers to promote integration through the arts. She was given the use of a music studio and gathered a group of participants together to write and produce a song. They advertised for local musicians to get involved and wrote a piece of music based around expressions of love in different languages. 'We wrote the song together and did everything from scratch. We have about twenty-five languages in the song and it was released in 2014. It's on Facebook, Soundcloud and YouTube. If there is one universal language it is music. Sometimes you don't speak the same language, but you can always dance, you can always move. Even if you don't have rhythm you can still move.'

After two years in direct provision, Mabel secured her refugee status and was given permission to remain in Ireland. 'I felt relieved because it meant I had freedom. I could go places, work and study. But the fact that I was living in direct provision never stopped me being social and meeting people.' She says residents in direct provision centres must show initiative by contacting local community groups and sharing their knowledge and expertise. 'Living in direct provision does not mean your legs have been cut off or your life is over. If you come here to be alive, then do it. If you want to get into the community, then go out there. You need to get up and do it for yourself. What's the worst that could happen? They'll tell you no. At least here nobody is going to stab you on the corner of the street or no one is going to shoot you on a public stage. At least you're sure of that.'

Finding paid employment in Sligo has not been easy for Mabel. She says every business in Sligo town has a copy of her CV. 'Initially when I came here I didn't know about the concept of volunteering from back in Cameroon. But I was told volunteering was a great way to help you up the work ladder. Now, nearly everything I do is volunteering because 80-90% of the time I don't hear back from employers. I don't like being idle so I'm at school studying business, office administration and Spanish at Sligo IT. I'm not going to sit here and wait for things to be given to me. I'm going to show people what I can do and what I can offer. And if they can pay me, all the better. But if you can't, I'll still be happy because this is what I love to do.'

She has considered packing her bags and leaving Sligo to find work in a larger town or city, but feels too connected to the local community to move away right now. She dismissed a friend's suggestion that using a more Irish name on her CV might make it easier to secure an interview. 'The priority is to go where I get work. If I get work in Sligo even better, I would totally stay there. I love it here. But if I don't find work I'll have to move. Whatever I thought I saw in my future, that whole perspective has changed since coming here. I would have arrived here thinking I'd love to work in advertising but then I realised there are other jobs that get you more involved with the human connection. I would love to work in culture and the arts.'

While she was still living in direct provision, Mabel was involved in setting up the Global Kitchen community cooking initiative. 'The main priority was to keep people occupied and get them out of the centre and meet other people. You may not be passionate about cooking but just come out. You might end up talking to someone who knows something about your interests and who could point you in the right direction.' Three years later, the Global Kitchen celebration of international food and culture still takes place every month. 'It started with just five people and now we cater for one hundred and fifty. We're looking at up-skilling people in different fields and sending them for courses so they can bring those skills back to the kitchen.' The end goal of the volunteer-run project is to provide paid employment for people when they leave direct provision. 'When people leave these centres they go where the work is. We're hoping this can become a social enterprise which would pay people to stay in Sligo.'

Mabel would also like to help bring more tourists to Sligo by using her marketing and advertising skills to promote her Irish hometown as an exciting destination. 'I read two weeks ago that Sligo was the least visited attraction on the Wild Atlantic Way and that broke my heart. So I think, I'm here, what can I do to help this situation? I've visited places where there's an avenue of shops with outdoor kitchens and open fire grills. We obviously don't have the weather for that here but we could build something similar with structures over them to keep the rain away. We could use the skills from Global Kitchen to attract more tourists.'

She recently applied for a visa for her mother to visit Ireland during the summer but the request was rejected.

She has suggested to her mother that she apply for family reunification in Ireland but she refuses to leave Cameroon, despite the growing unrest in the country's English-speaking regions. Her mother works as a weaver and up until recently made jumpers for children attending local schools. However, the decision in 2016 by English speaking teachers to close the schools and strike against the imposition of the French language in their curriculum has put a halt to education in the region. What began as protests and calls for greater recognition from the English-speaking minority had now descended into violent clashes between government forces and demonstrators. 'My mum's whole life is in Cameroon. But she's sitting there and getting no business. No one is talking about the schools resuming. The civil unrest is riling people up but I really hope it doesn't escalate because then my mother will have no choice and will have to leave. There is still some semblance of peace.'

For now, Mabel's volunteer work helps distract her mind from the loneliness of being so far from loved ones. 'I'm afraid if I stop working I'll think about being alone. But my positive experience in Sligo has made me almost not miss my family. My mum always asks how I've survived here and I tell her she just needs to come to Ireland. Then she'll understand.'

2014 Migration

In 2014 Syria overtook Afghanistan as the country with the world's largest number of refugees (an unenviable position Afghanistan had held for more than three decades). As the Syrian war entered its fourth year, the number of displaced people rose dramatically, with at least 7.6 million Syrians estimated to be displaced inside their own country. Globally the total number of people displaced as a result of persecution, conflict, violence or human rights violations rose to 59.5 million, roughly the same amount as the population of Italy or the United Kingdom.

Turkey became the largest refugee receiving country in the world with 1.59 million people, followed by Pakistan, Lebanon, Iran, Ethiopia and Jordan in that order. Despite the view held by some in Europe that the continent was in danger of becoming overrun by refugees, poor developing countries continued to host 86% of the world's displaced people. Nevertheless, numbers arriving into southern Europe did rise significantly in 2014, with more than 219,000 asylum seekers crossing the Mediterranean Sea, almost three times the number who crossed in 2011, the year of the Arab Spring.

Nearly half of those who arrived in 2014 had travelled either from Syria or Eritrea, a nation whose citizens continue to live under one of the world's most oppressive dictatorships. Faced with the prospect of indefinite national service in a country accused by the UN of carrying out 'systematic, widespread and gross human rights violations', hundreds of thousands of young people chose to flee north in the hopes of securing a safer life in Europe.[48]

In Syria and Iraq, the so-called Islamic State (IS)—the fundamentalist jihadist group, known as Daesh in Arabic—gained international notoriety after it released videotapes of the execution of two American journalists and a British aid worker. In June 2014 this group of extremist fighters, which had capitalised on the chaos in Syria and Iraq to take control of large swathes of both countries, declared it had created a 'caliphate' (a State under Islamic rule) and named the north-eastern Syrian city of Raqqa as its capital. In August a US-led coalition launched air strikes inside Iraq with the goal of destroying the movement. 'In a region that has known so much bloodshed, these terrorists are unique in their brutality,' said President Barack Obama in September. 'They execute captured prisoners. They kill children. They enslave, rape, and force women into marriage. They threaten a religious minority with genocide.'[49]

Meanwhile there were fears across Europe due to the increasing numbers of mainly young male westerners travelling from countries like France, the UK and Germany to join IS. By the end of 2014 it was estimated that between 11,000 and 15,000 foreign nationals were involved with IS in the conflict in Syria and Iraq, with concerns that Syrian war zones, in particular, were attracting men, and some women, from across Europe, North America and Australia. The German news magazine *Der Spiegel* reported in November 2014 that there were believed to be about one thousand French citizens in Iraq and Syria or en route to those countries; more than from any other European nation.

As war, terrorism, dictatorship and poverty in the Middle East and Africa continued to push up the numbers fleeing towards Europe, Italy made the decision to end its *Mare Nostrum* sea rescue mission. It announced that the mission had saved the lives of more than 100,000 migrants, but would be ended to make way for a smaller European Union scheme and to help relieve the strain on Italy's public finances. Human rights activists warned that with no alternative routes to Europe, the closure of *Mare Nostrum* was likely to lead to many more drownings. By the end of 2014 a total of 216,054 people had crossed the Mediterranean to seek asylum. Another 3,538 had died or gone missing in the attempt.

In Ireland, the Government announced the launch of the Syrian Humanitarian Admission Programme (SHAP)—a once-off and very limited private sponsorship scheme which would allow Irish citizens of Syrian birth and Syrian nationals lawfully resident in the country to bring family members either still in Syria, or living in refugee camps, to Ireland. The programme would be in addition to Ireland's established refugee resettlement programme which had been in operation since 2000 in collaboration with the UN Refugee Agency. Syrians living in Ireland (the sponsors) were given six weeks to apply for up to four family members to join them, with priority given to elderly parents, children, unaccompanied mothers and their children, single women, girls and disabled people. Family members admitted under the scheme would be allowed to work but if they could not find employment they would not be entitled to claim benefits. A total of 119 people were eventually reunited with family members through the programme.

For the first time since 2010 the number of applications for asylum in Ireland rose sharply in 2014, with 1,448 applications received, an increase of 53% on the previous year. The main nationalities to apply for refugee status were Pakistanis, Nigerians, Albanians, Bangladeshis and Zimbabweans. The overall number of non-EEA nationals with permission to remain in the State fell by 11% to 95,000, a decrease that could be attributed to the increasing number of people becoming naturalised citizens. Most of these were registered in Ireland to work or study, with the largest number coming from Brazil, followed by India, China, the USA, Nigeria and the Philippines.

In July, *The Irish Times* published a series of articles examining the lives of the 4,360 people living in 34 direct provision centres across the country. The series, entitled *Lives in Limbo,* reported that residents in these centres were spending years living in bleak, overcrowded and sometimes unhygienic conditions. It warned that being forced to live in these conditions, without being able to work, was damaging to the health, welfare and life-chances of asylum seekers. In October the Minister for Justice, Alan Shatter, announced the appointment of a Working Group under a retired High Court judge to report on how the direct provision could be improved. The McMahon report was published the following year in

June 2015 with over 170 recommendations which included improving the living conditions of direct provision centres and fast-tracking the granting of residency to people in the system five years or more.

The Irish Human Rights and Equality Commission called in December for a number of changes to the system including access to kitchens so that residents could prepare their own food, an increase in the weekly allowance to ensure 'dignity, respect and autonomy for individuals'—in 2014 an adult received €19.10 per week and a child €9.60 per week—and the provision of education and training for residents to prepare them for leaving the system and seeking employment. Geoffrey Shannon, the government's Special Rapporteur on Child Protection, warned that families in direct provision were living in restricted accommodation which could have a 'profound impact on the mental health of adults and children'. The children of asylum seekers were being forced to grow up in 'state-sanctioned poverty' with parents unable to adequately care for them. 'When we look back in 10 years' time, we may ask ourselves how we allowed the system to exist,' he went on 'The debate sparked by the Tuam mother and baby story should prompt us to reflect on the manner in which all children are treated in Ireland, not merely citizen children.'[50]

Flavia Camejo, 2014

Each morning at 7am Flavia Camejo used to travel across the city before work to visit the hospital morgue. There she would count the number of bodies laid out on stretchers before reporting back to the newsroom with the latest homicide death toll. 'There was never a single day when there were no bodies. I remember once I saw a guy with seventeen gunshots in his body. There were daily shootings between gangs. When you worked in Maracaibo as a journalist that was normal. I was only twenty years old then.'

Maracaibo, a city in north-western Venezuela, often features on lists of the most dangerous places in the world. This is where Flavia moved to study and work after she finished school. 'I had all the energy needed to be a journalist. I wanted to go out on the streets and talk to people. There had always been government control over what information was published in papers but I wanted to be an extra voice to what was going on in the country. I think the adrenalin of living in one of the most dangerous countries in the world just kept me going. But all the fear would hit me when I got home at the end of the day to my comfort zone. My mum would call every hour to see where I was and check if everything was OK. I suffered from anxiety but in Venezuela talking about anxiety is a taboo. Feeling nervous in Venezuela is normal. Being afraid is the norm.'

Flavia grew up in the small northern city of Coro, a place known for its warm weather and beautiful beaches. The grandchild of Italian immigrants who left Europe after the Second World War, Flavia spoke both Spanish and Italian at home. 'In Venezuela that's very common because after the war there were a lot of people who went to South America and Venezuela was one of their main destinations. Having those Italian roots makes me very proud. It was cool growing up with both those cultures.'

Despite her parents' attempts to shield their two daughters from the violence and corruption that plagued the country, Flavia was acutely aware of the dangers of everyday life in Venezuela. Watching her father double check the locks on the car doors every time the family left the house made his daughter increasingly apprehensive about the world outside the safety of the family home 'I think it was an awareness I developed after I was about ten years old. If my dad was driving, he would always look in the car mirrors to make sure nobody was following us. I have never felt safe in Venezuela to be honest. Even when I was growing up I could see the country was messed up. That's why I was a very nervous kid. I'm a nervous person in general but then I see my sister and realise she's exactly the same as me. So the pattern repeats itself.'

Flavia remembers when the military took to the streets following the attempted coup d'état in 2002. She regularly watched TV reports of protests around the country and would sit with her father each morning at breakfast to read the latest update in the newspaper. 'I remember seeing loads of military and army on the streets and I called them the men in green. My city was really small and before that you didn't see much action on the streets. You saw those kinds of things in films but you didn't expect to see them in real life. But then I began seeing videos on the TV of people being shot on the streets. One image that sticks in my mind is seeing the Venezuelan flag covered in blood on the street. After the coup things started to get a lot more dangerous in the country.' She remembers building up the courage to ask her parents about a news report on the kidnapping and murder of three children in Venezuela. 'As an eleven-year-old girl I didn't understand what the word kidnapping meant so I asked my dad. He tried to explain that there were bad people in the world and that we shouldn't give all our trust to people.'

Flavia's mother ran a hardware business, a trade that was common among Venezuela's middle-class Italian community. However, she feared because of her mother's success in developing the business, her family would be targeted by kidnappers. 'My family were not high class but you could never say out loud that my mum owned a business. People blamed you because you owned things.' Even at school, Flavia felt uncomfortable talking with friends about her parents' jobs. 'I think Chavez's speeches changed the way Venezuelan people saw the different classes. He wasn't only targeting big companies, he went for the small ones as well and the military would arrive at shops and close them down. You were always expecting the worst to happen. I was afraid of being kidnapped for what my mum did and what my family had.'

As Flavia grew up, the violence across Venezuela became increasingly widespread. She moved to Maracaibo for university and after graduating she applied for a journalism internship with one of the country's main newspapers. While living in Maracaibo, Flavia's fear of kidnapping became a reality. Her uncle, who was an engineer with a construction company, was seized by a group of men on his way into work. Flavia's aunt had only just given birth to a baby two months before her uncle was taken. He was held in an underground cell in the mountains for a week before he was found. 'They had a guard watching over him inside the cell with a massive gun, they were both living that same hell. When the police found him that man could have grabbed my uncle and shot someone. Luckily I think he was an amateur and my uncle was rescued.'

Flavia realises her uncle's strong business connections saved his life and that most other people in that situation would not have been so lucky. 'His family's contacts with the governor meant they brought in the special forces to help with his case. If that were another person they never would have done that. My uncle was never the same after the kidnapping. Before he was always very active and making jokes but he became quiet and his eyes seemed lost. He wouldn't speak. The family eventually left Venezuela and have been living in Panama for five years.'

Her uncle's kidnapping opened Flavia's eyes to risks of being a journalist. She enjoyed working in a bustling newsroom but often felt nervous when she was sent out on assignments following gangland shootings. 'What frightened me the most was not seeing the dead bodies but having to approach the families. In the newspaper where I worked they loved us to do follow up stories and would give me cases of guys who were shot by gangs. I would go to the neighbourhood and try to talk with people but they were always too afraid to speak and become involved in the case. Facing those people and learning more about those gangs, that was the really scary part.' Over time Flavia learned how to approach the families of deceased gang members and empathise with their suffering. 'It taught me how to speak to people and handle those types of situations. I'm very grateful for that because it prepared me for the rest of the time I spent working as a journalist in Maracaibo. And not only as a journalist but as a person.'

The more time she spent working within the Venezuelan media, it became impossible for Flavia to ignore the censorship that existed in news reporting, both before and after Hugo Chávez' death in 2013. She describes the paper she worked with in Maracaibo as 'softly pro-government'. They still made an effort to show both sides of the story but were more likely to cut stories from the opposition. She then returned to Coro where she worked for a strongly pro-government publication. 'Being such a small city you didn't have many options. I was coming from a massive newspaper in Maracaibo where the newsroom was incredible and the quality of the journalists was really impressive. In this newspaper in Coro you could see there was lots of money. The office was very modern and their salaries were very high. But then the reality kicked in that everything I had to write was related to the government.'

Flavia had already started thinking about leaving Venezuela when she moved back to Coro but didn't want to lose the journalistic skills she had established in Maracaibo. 'In fairness, I could have just worked with my mum's business and got some money from that but I didn't want to stop writing. I wanted to keep practising and go out on the streets and find news stories. I wanted to be the one telling people this is the reality in Venezuela.' However, when the Coro newspaper cut and completely re-worded an article she had written about anti-government demonstrators in the city, Flavia decided it was time to go. 'The reasons why I decided to leave was first because I wasn't feeling safe. What was the point in being a journalist when your life doesn't matter here? Secondly, it was the censorship. It made no sense being a journalist in Venezuela. Even the military are hitting back at them now. There's absolutely no protection at all for journalists.'

Flavia decided to use her Italian passport, which she was entitled to through her grandparents, to move to Europe and improve her English. She settled on Ireland, a country her mother had visited and fallen in love with as a teenager. In April 2014 she arrived in Dublin and quickly discovered many similarities between Irish people and her friends back home. 'In terms of personality, Irish people are so similar to Venezuelans. They are really friendly, talkative and always approach you to chat even when they know you're not from here. I think one of the most positive things about Irish people is they accept other nationalities and races.' For the first time in her life, Flavia felt comfortable walking down the street alone without the fear of being robbed or kidnapped. 'I don't remember walking much in Venezuela because it's so dangerous. It was such a contrast coming to Ireland from a country like Venezuela. '

Since arriving in Ireland three years ago, Flavia has witnessed the daily conversation in her extended family's WhatsApp group evolve from light chitchat into requests for bread and toothpaste. More recently, she has watched helplessly from afar as anti-government protests across Venezuela turned into violent clashes leaving hundreds injured and scores of people dead. 'I remember when the protests started I couldn't sleep at night and would wake from nightmares and grab my phone to call home and see if my family was OK. You could see the videos of the military shooting people and killing them when they're supposed to be protecting them. It was shocking to see how much the daily conversation between Venezuelan families changed. It went from normal stuff to "I don't have enough food" or "what can you exchange for toothpaste". These are the kind of conversations people in Venezuela have now.'

The chronic shortage of food and medical supplies across the country meant Flavia's father, who suffers from high blood pressure, was no longer able to buy his medication. The only way to purchase medication was to pay the exorbitant prices charged for supplies arriving from the Dutch island of Aruba on the black market, says Flavia. 'If you go into a pharmacy now it's completely empty. Whatever you're looking for, it's not there. The same thing is happening with food, the prices are so high. They're bringing food, medicine and even car parts in from Aruba but they sell them at a dollar rate which is very expensive.'

In 2017 Flavia's parents made the life-changing decision to leave Venezuela and follow her grandmother who the year before, after more than six decades in Latin America, had moved back to northern Italy. The family bought a small newsagents store in the touristic centre of Parma where Flavia's maternal grandmother is now living. Flavia's seventeen-year-old sister, who recently graduated from high school, will go to university in Italy. Her mother is accustomed to the Italian lifestyle but Flavia is worried about her father who has left his ninety-five-year-old mother behind in Venezuela. 'He doesn't really speak about it. He loves Italy and understands some Italian but he doesn't speak the language. We have always been a very close family so he was part of the Italian traditions but for him it's a massive change. He tries to keep it to himself but I know he's worried that he won't be able to see his mother again. I can see that he is sad and depressed. It's a big change to be making at his age.'

Flavia is very proud of the bravery her grandmother has shown in returning to a country she left more than six decades ago. 'I've always been very close to my granny, I'm actually named after her. She was only five years old when she moved to Venezuela and got married, created a family, had her own business and was happy. She embraced her new life in a very positive way and now if you ask her where she's from she says she's Venezuelan. I'm trying to follow her example because there is no going back. My granny has had to leave the country where she settled for us, for her future generations. Sadly, we have to repeat the history and embrace the exodus. In the past there were people from abroad coming to our country because we had opportunities. Now it's the other way around. People are actually leaving and running away because we have nothing. There's something very sad about that.'

Flavia now works for a tech company and plans to stay in Dublin. As an Italian passport holder, she is able to remain in Ireland without the stress of applying for visas. 'The fact that I'm half Italian and have a European passport has opened so many doors for me and given me opportunities that most other Venezuelans here wouldn't have. But at least 90% of Venezuelan immigrants are professionals with experience. Our type of immigration is quite different when you compare it with other nationalities.' She dreams of returning to Venezuela one day but worries she will find a very different place to the home she left. 'The best thing about Venezuela has always been the people. In Coro we have beautiful places but it's the people that make a country and all my people have left. My friends are all around the world now and even on my dad's side the family have gone to Panama, the US and Spain. I would love to go back and visit but I don't see myself living there again because I've become used to living a decent life. You actually get paid for your efforts here and can afford to rent a house or go on holiday. Venezuela is still in the past in that way.'

Flavia says most Venezuelans who have moved abroad for work or study tend to be overly patriotic about their home. 'Of course Venezuela is one of the most beautiful countries in the world but it doesn't mean it's the best. It's not and we need to be fair about that. We Venezuelans tend to be very blind. The land may be beautiful but our society is messed up.' She worries that people still living in Venezuela still cannot fully understand the political situation in their own country because of the government's control over the press. 'We know a lot about what's going on there but Venezuelans themselves have no idea. It's all blocked. There are so few TV channels and newspapers that belong to the opposition. Everything has a pro-government line. I feel frustrated by this. If I was still in Venezuela as a journalist I could be that extra voice, as I always wanted to be. The memories I have as a journalist in Venezuela are sweet and sour. Part of me would love to keep writing and

I still write in my free time. But it's not something I feel I have to do.'

Flavia now lives with her Irish boyfriend in south Dublin but struggles to answer when people ask her where home is. 'I don't really know anymore. I guess Ireland is home for me now. People say home is where your family is but my family is not in Venezuela anymore. The final part of this story is my family leaving Venezuela because we have nothing left there.' Flavia often turns to the memory of her great-grandmother for guidance when she feels lonely or misses Venezuela. 'She was the first woman in her region in Italy to hold the position of a local councillor but had to leave everything behind and go to Venezuela. She started from scratch and that's the kind of example I'm trying to follow. I have to build a life from zero here. That's why I always think of the women in my family as being very fierce.'

'I'm very happy here and I think I've got used to the country and its people very fast. There are so many opportunities here at the moment; I can't see myself anywhere else. People here complain about the weather and we understand that because we (Venezuelans) come from the tropics. But, we embrace the bad weather. We embrace the rain and the wind because, at the end of the day, even if it's raining outside, we're safe here.'

2015 Migration

'I never believed a photograph could have such an impact... People had seen a lot of other images from this war, but no image felt like the coming together of all those pictures and newsreels. It seems like everything culminated in that one picture.'[51]

In September 2015 Turkish photographer Nilufer Demir took a picture of a three-year-old Syrian refugee called Alan Kurdi lying face down and lifeless on a Turkish beach. For some reason, the image of a dead child on a faraway shore awoke people from their indifference to the migrant crisis unfolding across the Mediterranean. 'This picture wasn't taken in a war zone, it wasn't taken in Syria,' says Demir. 'The fact that this happened on a beach in Turkey has made people sit up and look.'[52]

2015 was the year Europeans began to pay attention. More than a million people arrived on Europe's southern shores that year, the vast majority risking their lives by crossing the Aegean Sea to Greece. More than 3,700 died or went missing crossing the sea. Hundreds of thousands of these—mainly Syrians and Iraqis—continued their odyssey on foot, embarking on an often equally hazardous journey through the Balkans and across mainland Europe, prompting images reminiscent of the flood of refugees displaced by World War II.

Germany responded by generously opening its doors to these weary travellers. In September, German Chancellor Angela Merkel and Austrian Chancellor Werner Faymann granted passage to 10,000 refugees stranded in Hungary. Merkel said it was Germany's 'damned duty' to be taking in 'people who are running for their lives'. Defending her open-door policy, the German Chancellor described the migrant crisis as a 'historic test' for Europe. 'Something that was far away from us—that we have seen on television—is now literally at our front door. The war in Syria, the barrel bombings, the spread of IS in Syria and Iraq … all that is no longer far away but has come to us.' By the end of the year over a million asylum seekers had registered in Germany.

Hungary's response to the influx of refugees was very different, with Prime Minister Viktor Orban signing off on the construction of a razor-topped fence along its nation's 175 kilometre border with Serbia. Meanwhile in the UK British Prime Minister David Cameron was harshly criticised after he described migrants as 'a swarm of people coming across the Mediterranean'. The Labour party's Harriet Harman reminded the prime minister that he was talking about people, 'not insects', and warned that the use of 'divisive language' had taken a 'worrying turn'.

France was also affected. Hundreds of asylum seekers had reached the 'jungle' camp in Calais in northern France, desperate to cross to England by whatever means possible (with some losing their lives in the attempt). David Cameron said the UK would not become a 'safe haven' for such migrants. He told the BBC 'everything that can be done will be done to make sure our borders are secure.' The UK *Daily Mail* sympathised with British holidaymakers and lorry drivers sitting 'petrified' in their vehicles with windows and doors locked shut as 'migrants brazenly try to clamber aboard'. 'The Calais shambles may have been building for months, but make no mistake: we are now witnessing a crisis which is having devastating repercussions across Britain,' wrote the *Mail*.[53]

In Ireland one of the country's foremost businessmen, Peter Sutherland—who was also the UN Secretary General's Special Representative for International Migration—called on the government to open the nation's doors to more people fleeing war and persecution. 'Ireland has the—I won't say unique—but rather positive position that we don't have a racist, anti-immigrant party,' he told RTÉ news in July of that year. 'We don't have a political movement of the toxic kind that you find in so many other countries and I think we can be proud of that and that we should take more refugees rather than less.'

The UN's Special Rapporteur on the Human Rights of Migrants Francois Crépeau sent a strong rebuke to EU leaders. 'Let's not pretend that what the EU and its member states are doing is working. Migration is here to stay. Building fences, using tear gas and other forms of violence against migrants and asylum-seekers, detention, withholding access to basics such as shelter, food or water and using threatening language or hateful speech will not stop migrants from coming or trying to come to Europe.'

2015 was also what the *Financial Times* called 'France's year of terror':[54] the January attack on the *Charlie Hebdo* magazine's Paris office, which left ten journalists and two policemen dead, was followed in November by a wave of attacks in the French capital when gunmen and suicide bombers struck the Bataclan concert hall, the Stade de France and restaurants and bars, leaving 130 dead and hundreds wounded. French president Francois Hollande described the November attack as an 'act of war' by Islamic State, while EU leaders called for a clampdown on free movement across borders after a Syrian passport was found near the body of one of the attackers.

In September 2015 Ireland responded to the wave of European public and political concern caused by the Alan Kurdi photo by agreeing to accept up to 4,000 asylum seekers from refugee camps in Greece, Lebanon, Jordan and Italy by the end of 2017 under the new Irish Refugee Protection Programme. The Department of Justice announced that emergency reception centres would be established for the new arrivals: such centres opened in the Hazel Hotel in Monasterevin, Co Kildare and Clonea Strand Hotel in Dungarvan, Co Waterford in 2016, followed by the Abbeyfield Hotel in Ballaghaderreen, Co Roscommon in 2017.

In May 2015 the naval service flagship LE Eithne left for the Mediterranean to take part in Ireland's first ever humanitarian mission in international waters as part of the EU Triton search-and-rescue initiative. The ship's role was to rescue people risking their lives by crossing the Mediterranean in unseaworthy vessels and bringing them to shore, usually in Italy. By July 2017, the Defence Forces would have rescued nearly 16,000 migrants.

Meanwhile Irish people, motivated by the images on their TV screens to do something for the hundreds of thousands of people trudging across Europe, took matters into their own hands by pledging beds, rooms and houses through advocacy groups like Uplift. Uplift ran a 'pledge a bed' campaign, saying it gave ordinary people the chance to show 'the humanity and decency that our politicians are too cowardly to. With the images we are seeing, people cannot sit and do nothing any more. There is a hunger to do something to help and this is a powerful way of showing solidarity'. The Irish Red Cross was given the role of vetting the offers and spent the following year sifting through pledges of accommodation, goods and services across Ireland. However it would be 2017 before the first handful of refugees began moving into Irish homes.

As the economy began to improve, the number of newly arrived immigrants, including students and economic migrants, increased to 79,300 by April 2016, while there were 114,000 non-EEA nationals with permission to remain in the country at the end of the year. The number of applications for refugee status in Ireland rose by 126% in 2015 to 3,276, with the highest number coming from Pakistan, Bangladesh, Albania, Nigeria and India. There were a total of 4,696 people living in the direct provision system by the end of 2015. A report into improvements to the protection process, chaired by retired High Court judge Bryan McMahon and published in June, recommended that newly arrived asylum seekers should have a decision on their application within twelve months and should be given the right to work after nine months. The report also noted that 'as a matter of principle', no one should spend more than five years in the direct provision system.

2015 was the year of the refugee. The images of pain and death we had witnessed on our TV screens in faraway countries like Syria were no longer detached from our daily lives. The suffering had reached our doorsteps. In the words of António Guterres, UN High Commissioner for Refugees (and later to become UN Secretary General), Europe was now facing 'an unchecked slide into an era in which the scale of global forced displacement as well as the response required is clearly dwarfing anything seen before.'

Ellen Baker and James Sweeney, 2015

James Sweeney was standing beside the ruins of a nineteenth-century stone cottage outside the village of Easkey in Co Sligo the first time he felt a real connection to his ancestral home. Placing his hand on the cold, damp stone walls of the ruined building, he tried to imagine the bustle of nineteen brothers and sisters growing up inside the small building. In 1884 James's grandfather Owen Sweeney left this cottage and emigrated to New York in search of a better life. There he met Katherine Dolphin, a woman who had also emigrated from Co Sligo and the couple were married in 1898. Almost exactly one hundred years later, James made his first trip to Ireland with his wife Ellen Baker to investigate his Irish roots. Ellen was also eager to learn about the woman she was named after— her great-grandmother Ellen Moriarty from Cahersiveen in Co Kerry. 'We're all made of stardust,' says Ellen. 'When you come back to where your family's DNA is, there's just something there. I think that's why it was so easy for us to make the decision to move here. It was the most natural thing in the world.'

In May 2015, James and Ellen sold their home in Tarrytown on the banks of the Hudson River, north of New York City, and relocated to Dublin where they now live in an apartment on the banks of the Grand Canal. As you step inside their Dublin home you're greeted with the story of their life. A vibrant art collection covers the walls and family photographs are dotted around the rooms. They spent a year sifting through their belongings before leaving and gave most things away. The rest was packed into boxes and shipped across the Atlantic.

Before the move, James and Ellen had spent most of their lives in New York. 'With New York City it's a love-hate relationship,' says Ellen, who grew up on the Upper East Side. 'It's hard to live in New York and it's very expensive. I never lived in the city for very long once I was an adult.' James, who was born in Brooklyn and raised in Queens, got a job when he was in his twenties at the Montefiore Medical Center where he worked for exactly forty years. He started off in the bio-engineering department of the hospital before moving into anaesthesiology as a medical systems engineer. Ellen, born in Manhattan, dropped out of college where she was studying theatre when she was twenty-one. She moved onto secretarial work and spent the following ten years working on Wall Street while finishing her bachelor's degree on the weekends and eventually set up her own business in bookkeeping and accounting. 'I went back to school and I got an MBA with an emphasis on accounting. I began to learn bookkeeping and loved it. There was just something about it that appealed to me because it's so orderly. That's the way I like to live my life. I can live only in the present moment but I like to know where everything is and I want it all to fit into place. I want a beginning, a middle and an end. I started my own business and had it for twenty-five years. It was probably the most gratifying way I ever could have worked.'

The couple began dating in the mid-90s and were married just over a year later. Although they no longer lived in the city when it happened, the events of September 2001 deeply affected them on a personal level. James's sister, Rita, had recently retired from the Port Authority of New York which had built the World Trade Center and had offices on the site. Ellen was on the phone to her sister-in-law watching the disaster unfold on live television when the twin towers collapsed. 'Rita was chatting about the facts to Ellen, saying the building was built to withstand such a collision and planes had been known to fly into buildings before,' says James. 'She was at the point of telling Ellen that the building would sustain the impact when the thing collapsed. So yes, it was personal. We lost a cousin, my mother's cousin, she was working in one of the firms there.'

James arrived at work in the Bronx that morning into a hospital preparing for disaster. 'We expected casualties but they never came. It's a type of disaster where there aren't too many casualties. You either get away or you don't.' Meanwhile, Ellen was worried about her mother. 'My mother was a die-hard New Yorker, wild horses couldn't drag her out of Manhattan. She had just moved into a retirement home in Battery Park, four blocks from the World Trade Center.' Ellen spoke to her mother shortly after the first plane hit the north tower but lost communication after the phone lines stopped working. She spent the next few hours anxiously waiting for news from the retirement home as she watched the chaos in Lower Manhattan unfold on the television. Eventually they called to say all the residents had been evacuated to a home in the Bronx. Ellen waited for James to return home before the couple drove into the city to pick her up. 'She only lived a year after that,' says

Ellen. 'She hardly survived it, she was so shook up. The next few days she was hallucinating. She said there were bombers, she was re-living the war. It was awful for her.'

Like most New Yorkers, Ellen and James spent a long time coming to terms with the events of 9/11. They decided to focus their energies on the future and began planning trips abroad. The couple had visited Ireland for the first time the year before the New York attacks and were eager to spend more time in their ancestral home. 'I've done a certain amount of travelling and I'd have to say that the only travelling that's worthwhile is when you actually spend time with the people,' says James. 'You can go on a tour and sit on a bus and you're in a bubble but when you actually spend time with people, you learn about their culture. And that understanding had become deeper here because of my family.'

As the years passed and retirement started to loom on the horizon, Ellen and James began discussing the possibility of moving full time to Ireland. 'We knew we would not be able to maintain a large house as we grew older and property taxes are so high and continue to rise unabated where we lived,' says Ellen. 'We were concerned about driving as we aged and wanted to settle somewhere we did not need a car. The cold, snowy winters were not a compelling reason to stay in the area either.' The re-election of George Bush Jr as US president in 2004 was also a push factor in the couple's decision to move abroad. 'We were looking at our retirement and thinking about life in the US beyond sixty-five. What would be available to us in terms of social services? This crazy Congress and right-wingers were ready to shut down Medicare. With real estate taxes going up where we lived, there was no end in sight.' 'I think what we wanted was the challenge of being able to live in another culture and to learn from that experience,' says James. 'We didn't want to just be comfortable and settle down into what we had.'

James had already secured Irish citizenship through his grandfather and in 2005 Ellen also applied for citizenship. At first, the couple planned to settle in the countryside, but a love of Dublin changed their minds. 'We loved Dublin because it was like a mini New York but without all the downsides of New York,' says Ellen. 'Some of the neighbourhoods reminded me of places in the upper west side. The energy here, the feeling of the city and the whole vibe is so New York but it's cleaner, friendlier, smaller, cheaper. It's like a mini version of any other great city.' Ellen and James spent a long time planning and researching before finally making the move. 'We were realistic about the differences between the two countries,' says Ellen. 'We did our homework and lots of consulting on housing, finances, taxes and medical care. We have cousins in Dublin too and they were invaluable in helping us with logistics.'

After months of preparations, Ellen and James arrived in Ireland on their wedding anniversary, 4 May 2015. James had researched courses in veterinary science and was accepted into the Dún Laoghaire Further Education Institute to study Animal Health Care. 'I had the aspiration to fulfil a dream I've always had. I've worked in healthcare all my life but I was always on the non-clinical side.' He enjoyed the programme but was unable to find work experience which was a mandatory element of the course. 'Finding work experience was near nigh impossible. Students had it pretty much sewn up a year in advance. It's so competitive to find places, so I had to leave the school.' James found volunteer work at Dublin Zoo, helping out with special events and tours. 'It's mostly education, taking groups around for walks and talks. We have a discovery centre and then conservation talks with the kids. Zoos are like a conservation oasis in the world today, holding on to the things that are rapidly disappearing for the environment itself.'

He also volunteers every Thursday night with the Irish Blue Cross mobile clinic in Finglas as a veterinary assistant. 'The vet himself is Slovakian and he has a day job and this is his second job at night. Mostly I do book keeping, keep track of the records as people come in, note the medications that are used and assist with the vet. I've found real satisfaction in volunteering for Dublin Zoo as well as the Irish Blue Cross. So much so that I started taking distance-learning classes in a veterinary technician course through a college in New Mexico. It's a one year veterinary assistant level course that continues into a full veterinary technician course which is probably equivalent to the veterinary nursing done here.'

Ellen volunteers as a tour guide in St Patrick's Cathedral every Wednesday afternoon and helps out at the Oxfam bookshop on Parliament Street. 'You spend a lot of time in Oxfam talking with people about different things. Especially when you're talking about books, that's easy. I started out by just filling in for people who were away and finally they put me on the roster.' She also recently started a third volunteer job with Youth Work Ireland. People often ask Ellen whether she would consider returning to accounting and finding work as a bookkeeper. 'I did that for twenty-five years and I really enjoyed it but I knew it was coming to an end one day. It's like being in secondary school; you don't want to be there forever. I don't ever want to work again for money because once somebody pays me they own me. Having the freedom of not having to depend on what I do every day to pay for food is wonderful.'

The couple were surprised by how quickly they settled into a new Dublin routine. 'It's been the most natural transition in the world,' says Ellen. 'I went into therapy for a year before we moved because I was worried about the sleepless nights and what ifs. But Ireland has a way of weaving you in. For me it's been a no brainer.' The couple sing with the Revenue choir and Ellen is a member of an interfaith women's organisation which promotes dialogue and acceptance among people of different religions. 'I've found it easy to make friends. Well, acquaintances that lead ultimately to friendships. I don't say no to anything and I take every opportunity I can to meet new people.' James says most of their new friends in Dublin are through Ellen. 'Volunteering work, even in the States, is mostly done by women and I think the opportunity for men to meet through volunteering situations is not as robust.'

In May 2017, the couple visited the United States for the first time since their move two years previously. Having left their country during the Obama administration, it was strange and unsettling to return to a nation dominated by news on Donald Trump's never-ending and increasingly unpredictable tweets from the White House. 'It was sort of like a litmus test going back to the States and observing how I felt about being there, and then how I felt when we came back,' says James. 'I thought to myself how lucky I am to be at a point in my life where I can retire and live in a community of people who try to work together on the same page rather than the antagonism that we had left behind.'

During the trip James quickly tired of the never-ending TV reports on Trump's latest hiccup or international faux-pas. 'News over in the States is a constant drum beat. You go into a diner or into a store and there's a TV on and it's invariably showing the news.' Ellen admits to feeling a sort of 'survivor's guilt' for leaving the country before Trump was elected president. 'If there's one person I really feel for and wish I could rescue out of there it would be my niece. She's in Los Angeles and she's the closest thing I have to my own child. She's got her whole life ahead of her. I know now what it feels like for parents who ask "what am I leaving behind for my children?"' James is trying to focus on the prospect that Trump's stay in office will be temporary and that eventually he will be replaced. However, he still worries about the long-term implications of the business mogul's policy decisions. 'For all that Trump is boss now, he'll be gone at some point. It will be interesting to see who replaces him and what lessons the country has learned from his presidency. But my big concern is that, from an environmental perspective, the world can't wait on these rolls of the dice and I'm hoping we just don't run out of time.'

Living so far from friends in the US has been made a lot easier for Ellen and James through online tools like WhatsApp and Skype. However, meeting friends and family face-to-face during their recent trip back to the States felt far more powerful and meaningful than any phone call or internet chat. 'It was nice to just be with people,' says James. 'Yes, you can be on the phone and have a Skype connection or Facetime but to actually be with somebody in a room, there's a totally different chemistry there.' One close friend lost her sister to cancer while Ellen and James were visiting. 'We had known her very well and she had liver cancer. We were there when she passed away and we went to the funeral. We grieved with them and talked with them, we were physically there for them. That's not something you can do over the phone.'

Before returning to Ireland, Ellen arranged to have dinner with a group of women friends who she has known for twenty-five years. 'We used to get together about four to five times a year for dinner and it would just be a really special event. I know eventually I will have long-term deep connections with friends I have made in Ireland but I just wish I could move my US and Irish friends to the same city. With my American friends it's a twenty-five-year friendship, a deep connection. I do miss that.'

James says the month back in the States only reaffirmed their decision to move to Ireland. 'I could never imagine living there now as a retired person compared to the richness that we have here and the access to culture. It's just the overall attitude of people here, there's more of a cohesiveness and purpose. People are working with each other and trying to make life work. Even in the New York area there is this coldness to the way people live and I think it's gotten worse under the Trump presidency. The constitution of the United States set up a democracy and I think that's still an ongoing experiment. In my youth there was always a feeling of the country pushing forward. Now we're seeing a country where people want to go in different directions. You had the Obama administration which had one vision and now you have the Trump administration which has an entirely different vision. To see a country with such divergent approaches is a bit distressing. I can't see what good is going to come from this.'

He is also tired of hearing constant claims that the United States is the greatest country on earth. 'I learned a long time ago that when you think you're the best and the brightest you're setting yourself up for a fall. And that's all you ever hear in the United States, that we're the greatest country in the world; that we have the biggest guns, the most money, the smartest people and the greatest schools. What are people learning from that? There's no sense of humility there. We're all human and we're all flawed. The US just has a really big ego.'

Spending a month back in the United States actually made Ellen feel more at home in Ireland. 'There's definitely something that's shifted slightly in me since we came back. It's not anything positive or negative, it's just some funny little change. I no longer feel like when I walk out the door people are looking at me and saying "oh, she's a foreigner". Dublin's absolutely home.' Ellen is still trying to find out more information about her great-grandmother's family in Co Kerry and sometimes feels envious of James' direct link to Ireland through his grandfather. 'I have connections here but they're another generation back and they're basically lost. I keep asking myself, when are you going to start feeling like you're one of them in terms of your Irish heritage? I know I'm Irish because I have a passport but I have to remind myself I'm a citizen here and that I'm Irish in my blood.'

While she has failed to uncover any living relatives in Ireland, Ellen has no regrets about making the move. 'I had no idea the incredible influence that Ireland has on people with Irish heritage. You come here and it's like "I understand your brain and your sense of humour". Ireland has a way of drawing you in. We had a dream, we made a plan and then we jumped in the water. Trust, trust, trust. Anyone can learn how to swim.'

2016 Migration

The first major shock of 2016 came on the morning of 24 June. The people of the United Kingdom had fallen asleep the night before to the news that Nigel Farage, leader of UKIP—the Eurosceptic far-right UK Independence Party—had conceded defeat in the Brexit referendum. A YouGov poll published at 10pm had put Remain four points ahead. However the final result was not what the polls had predicted—51.9% voted in favour of leaving the European Union while 48.1% voted to remain. After more 43 years, one of Europe's three most powerful nations had decided it was time to leave the EU.

Four and half months later, on the other side of the Atlantic, the polls got it utterly wrong once again. This time it was the victory of a bragging, bullying extremist, a man who somehow—even after accusations of sexual assault and collusion with Russia—succeeded in shattering practically all expectations in becoming the forty-fifth president of the United States. Donald Trump ran a campaign which associated immigrants with crime, terrorism and threats to American jobs, compounding pre-existing fears over border security, refugee admissions and immigration from Muslim countries. Trump's win sent aftershocks rippling across the globe.

Suddenly the policies and rhetoric of the right-wing anti-immigration groups spreading across Europe were gaining momentum. 'This was the year of the populist revolt,' wrote Ruadhán Mac Cormaic in *The Irish Times* in December 2016. 'Around Europe, right wing anti-establishment parties are on the march. Their policy platforms may vary… but what they share is a broadly protectionist economic agenda, nativist social polices and a simple, well-honed message that pits a corrupted metropolitan elite against the ordinary, forgotten citizen.'[55]

This new wave of populism viewed the Brexit and Trump victories as a revolt against the 'privileged minorities', writes Ivan Krastov. 'In the rhetoric of populist parties, elites and migrants are twins who thrive off of one another: neither is like 'us', both steal and rob from the honest majority, neither pays the taxes that it should pay, and both are indifferent or hostile to local traditions.'[56]

Migrants fleeing war and poverty, continued to arrive into the European Union throughout 2016, albeit in smaller numbers than the previous year—362,453 people arrived in Europe by sea in 2016 compared to over a million arrivals in 2015. In March the European Union reached an agreement with Turkey to try and resolve irregular migration across the Aegean Sea into Greece. Under this agreement, all illegal migrants crossing the sea from Turkey to the Greek islands would be returned to Turkey. For every Syrian migrant returned to Turkey, another Syrian waiting in Turkey would be resettled in Europe. Turkey also promised to take the necessary steps to prevent the creation of any new sea or land routes into Europe, while the EU promised to speed up Turkey's accession process into the Union.

Human rights groups across Europe responded to the controversial accord with outrage, arguing that refugees in

Greece were being sent back to Turkish internment camps with the additional fear that Syrian refugees could be deported back to Syria. The Irish Human Rights and Equality Commission (IHREC) warned that the EU-Turkey agreement risked placing the EU in direct violation of the principle of non-refoulement (the prohibition against returning asylum seekers to a country where they risk persecution). 'Instead of greater solidarity, we are now pushing those responsibilities back further through returns to Turkey and its designation as a safe third country,' said the IHREC, adding that migrant children, in particular, were at serious risk under the new system.[57]

In Syria the conflict so many of these people were fleeing had continued into its sixth year with an estimated 470,000 people dead and 11 million forced from their homes. Behind these statistics lay the stories of tens of thousands of families torn apart by the conflict with countless innocent civilians killed or injured. In 2016 at least 652 children were killed in the conflict, according to a report from Unicef. 'No child is spared the horror of the war in Syria, where children come under attack on a daily basis,' warned the charity. 'Violence is everywhere, ripping apart places that children thought were safe—places that should be safe: schools, hospitals, playgrounds, public parks and children's own homes. Children have paid the heaviest price in this six-year war.'[58]

The situation for asylum seekers living in the Calais 'jungle' refugee camp seriously deteriorated after the French government deployed more than 1,200 police officers in October to clear the camp and raze its makeshift shanty town to the ground. An estimated 6,000-8,000 people were living in the camp before it was demolished. Local officials reported that some 5,000 migrants were transported from the rubble in buses to centres in 450 locations around France, while a small number remained in the area determined to reach Britain.

In Ireland the number of asylum applications dropped slightly to 2,244 from the 3,276 applications received the previous year. The main nationalities of first time applications for refugee status were Syria, Pakistan, Albania, Zimbabwe and Nigeria. A total of 4,425 people were living in direct provision centres by the end of the year with people spending an average of three years in the system, down from four years in 2014. These centres were separate to the Emergency Reception and Orientation Centres which opened in 2016 to house approved Syrian 'programme refugees' from camps in Greece and Lebanon. Initial arrivals under the resettlement and relocation programme were sent to the Hazel Hotel in Monasterevin, Co Kildare and Clonlea Strand Hotel in Dungarvan, Co Waterford. Others were sent to stay in direct provision centres such as Mosney in Co Meath.

The International Protection Act 2015, which had been signed into law the previous year, came into effect on 31 December. While the new system sought to streamline the application process for asylum seekers, refugee support groups warned that the act was an 'erosion of family reunification rights'. Under the Act, refugees could only apply for an existing spouse or child under 18 to join them in Ireland. This meant that elderly parents, same-sex partners, adult children and those in civil partnerships would be excluded from the family reunification process.

A total of 115,000 non-EEA nationals were living in Ireland by the end of 2016; the majority of these came from Brazil, India, China, the USA and Pakistan. Non-Irish nationals from outside the EU accounted for 34.8 % of the total number of immigrants to arrive in Ireland in 2016, down from 40% the previous year. Returning Irish nationals were the largest immigrant group to Ireland while the total number of newly arriving immigrants coming to Ireland for work and study—including people from both in and outside the EU—increased to 84,600.

Internationally, the fear of the outsider only gained strength in 2016, particularly following the Brussels terrorist attack in March which left 31 people dead and 220 injured, and the Bastille Day attack in Nice on 14 July, when a lorry driven by a man from Tunisia ploughed into a large crowd watching a fireworks display, killing 86 people and injuring hundreds, including children. The year's attacks only reinforced the belief being spread by populist parties that increased immigration would lead to more terror attacks. However, a UN report from the Special Rapporteur on the promotion and protection of human rights warned that further attempts to crackdown on migration and restrictive immigration policies could in fact worsen the risk of more attacks across Europe.

The report argued that there was little evidence of terror groups using refugee flows to enter Europe or that asylum seekers were more prone to radicalisation, but warned that migration policies that build fences and abandon international legal commitments to refugees could create conditions that would ultimately 'lead to increased terrorist activity'. 'We are here today to correct the misperception that international refugee law is an obstacle when it comes to addressing security concerns,' said Ben Emmerson, UN Special Rapporteur on counter-terrorism and human rights, in October. 'In fact, it is in all of our interests to protect refugees and give them the opportunity to create a better future for themselves and their families. It is also the right thing to do.'[59]

Maisa Al-Hariri, 2016

The first time Maisa Al-Hariri saw a news report about the boats crossing the Mediterranean packed with hundreds of asylum seekers, she never imagined her own family would end up on one of those rickety rafts. The young student had already been forced to leave her home in Syria and was still coming to terms with her family's move to Istanbul. 'We heard that people were going abroad across the sea but I couldn't believe that we would ever cross that way. I saw it on the TV and internet and it looked so scary.'

The family left their home in the city of Daraa in southwestern Syria in January 2015 and travelled to Turkey where Maisa's father had already arrived to make arrangements for his wife, daughters and son. Daraa, which sits close to the Jordanian border and south of the Syrian capital of Damascus, was just like any other big city before the war broke out, says Maisa.

'There were always festivals and every Friday neighbours would get together to celebrate the end of the week. We were always going out to the parks for picnics. People would gather together a lot. Syria is a country rich in history and there were so many places to visit for tourists. Everything was easy back then. People were happy. Families and relatives were all together. It was our homeland.'

When the conflict broke out in Daraa, Maisa and her friends believed the bombings would end within a few weeks. 'We didn't think it would reach our home or continue for so long. But it carried on into years and finally the time came when we had to decide to leave. We didn't have a future there any more, everything had been destroyed.' What she once knew as a city of harmony and co-existence had become a perilous place where neighbours no longer trusted each other for fear of being denounced to the authorities. 'There was a lot of questioning by police and trust between friends fell apart which was really hard. People couldn't believe in each other. Even neighbours entering each other's homes were careful.

'We were all Syrian but suddenly people were asking "Which city are you from?", "Who do you support?", You never knew if the person in front of you was with the government or the opposition. There was so much tension and people were afraid for their children. My mum was so worried about us, we couldn't live there anymore.'

Her father had already spent a year in Turkey when he arranged for his wife and children to travel north and join him. Maisa and her younger sisters were enrolled in a local school in Istanbul where she completed her final year of secondary education. However, she found that the Turkish school system discriminated against Syrian refugees and was unable to find a university that would accept her results. 'I hated myself because I couldn't work and I couldn't learn the Turkish language. The schools for Syrians were temporary and were not in a good way. The education system was messy. It was not important to the Turkish government that Syrians entered university. We also had to study Turkish, which was very hard for people coming from a country with a completely different language. Nothing was taken seriously in the schools. The teacher would just come in, give the class and leave. They made people feel like education was not important. After school a person would just go and work as anything with a very low salary just to pay for their living.'

In Syria, Maisa and her siblings had studied at a private school where subjects were taught through English. Her parents, who both worked as lecturers in the university in Daraa, were eager for their children to speak the language fluently. 'My mother had seen difficulties in her own family and wanted us to have a better future. She herself had faced many troubles in her life and wanted the best for us. English and French are both used in Syria but I did English because I liked it more.'

In October 2015, Maisa's twenty-four-year-old sister became the first member of the family to risk crossing the Mediterranean. She left Turkey to join the tens of thousands of others travelling across mainland Europe in the hopes of finding stability and safety in countries like Germany, the UK and Sweden. 'She was so brave and we were really afraid for her. But she crossed at the time when all the borders were still open and walked across Europe to Belgium. She walked with families who could support her.'

Meanwhile, back in Turkey, Maisa's mother Fatima began making arrangements for herself and her daughters to make the treacherous crossing to Greece. Her father and brother decided to stay in Turkey as they had both found employment. The family also decided that Maisa's youngest sister Amira, who was thirteen at the time, would stay in Istanbul with her father. 'It was too dangerous for her to come and my mum was afraid for her. We didn't think we would survive the crossing. I didn't want to go and kept on delaying the journey. They were stopping Syrians from going from Istanbul to Izmir and it was getting really strict.'

On the afternoon of 18 March 2016, Maisa and her family were at a friend's house in Istanbul when they received word from a smuggler that it was time to leave. 'He said we had to go right away. I couldn't believe it and was not prepared at all. I didn't have anything with me. We didn't know anything about the new rules in Greece and that they were holding people on the islands.'

The family had paid $1,500 for three people—Maisa, her mother and her older sister Taqwa—to cross to the Aegean Sea to the Greek islands, but convinced the smuggler to allow a fourth person, Maisa's younger sister Sarra, to come along. Conscious of the long journey that lay ahead, the women packed two small bags with one change of clothes for each of them and a file containing their identity papers and educational certificates. They were brought to a bus that took them, and about 40 other Syrians, from Istanbul to the coastal city of Izmir. 'It was very dangerous even travelling between Istanbul and Izmir from where the boat would leave. The smuggler was trying not to let the police catch us. At that point I still didn't believe it was going to happen, I thought we would go back to Istanbul. I couldn't accept that we were actually leaving.'

The bus arrived in the Turkish coastal city at 9am, too late for the early morning crossing to Greece. The men, women and children on board the bus were told they would have to wait till dark before setting out across the sea. 'That morning it started raining and it was really very cold. The smuggler was not there with us and we had to wait the whole day in the mud with no food. It was such a tense day, every second that passed felt like a year. At midnight they told us to get ready, that we were leaving.'

Maisa's family had paid an extra fee for lifejackets and slung them over their heads while a couple of men pumped air into a small inflatable raft. The group was then packed onto the dingy which floated precariously by the water's edge. 'Everyone was shouting and the kids were afraid. How were they going to fit such a big number of people onto that tiny raft filled with air? There were about six children in the group and it was so hard thinking about that cold sea and what could happen to us.'

Once everyone had squeezed onto the raft, the group set off towards the distant lights of Lesvos twinkling on the horizon. However, it quickly became apparent that there was a leak in the boat with water slowly seeping through the rubber. 'It was completely dark. The water was coming inside the boat and I couldn't see my sisters. We could only hear each other's voices. My mum was sitting in the back, where it got really wet. When we reached the middle of the sea the raft was no longer moving, it felt like we were stuck. Those three hours felt like an age. I was just praying to God that we would reach safety. We could always see the lights on the island but it was so far away.'

Shortly before 4am, the raft landed on a beach on the island of Lesvos. NGO staff and volunteers were waiting for the group to arrive and offered them dry clothing once they came ashore. Having spent more than three hours in a water-logged vessel,

Maisa's mother was unable to walk up the beach. 'My mum was in a very bad situation. She couldn't move her legs at all, they were completely jammed. I was so scared we would lose her. But God gave her another life and I'm so happy for that. Without her we would have never reached here.'

The girls and their mother were brought to a refugee camp on the island and registered two days later. However, life in the centre was chaotic and the women were emotionally and physically exhausted after their journey from Turkey. 'It was a new experience. I'd never lived in a camp before and no one could tell us what was going on. We just saw what other people were doing and followed them. We spent one month in that camp, it was really tough. There wasn't enough food for us and some people were getting really angry. Two or three times there were fires in the camp. People would protest by not eating and said they wanted to leave the island.'

Eventually, the Al-Hariri women were transferred to a family camp on the island and soon afterwards their registration papers arrived. Maisa began working as an interpreter, helping NGOs communicate with refugees across the island. 'I was given a proper card like I was legal person so I could move around and visit Athens. Everything started to change from that day. I worked with different organisations and used to sit with volunteers as a translator helping anyone who asked for information. It was a Greek organisation for housing families in a severe situation. In another camp I worked with the Humanitarian Support Agency and helped with clothing distribution.' The work helped distract Maisa from her family's predicament and the uncertainty around their future in Europe. 'I was always positive at that time about everything.

I was there to help people and knew that God would help me with my papers. At times I asked myself why has this happened to me, but then I felt my heart telling me everything will be fine. We would find a good place in the end and we wouldn't stay in Greece.'

As the months passed Maisa witnessed at first hand the growing unrest in the camps and was eager for her family to get out of Greece. 'Before we left things started to get extremely bad. It's full of mafia now and it was very dangerous for single women. Anything could happen—like stealing and drugs— and some women, if they didn't find food, they had to sell themselves for money. Thank god our family never had to stay on the street.' Maisa was also conscious that her family had arrived in Greece just two days after the EU-Turkey agreement was announced. Under the deal, illegal migrants who arrived by sea would be sent back to Turkey. Fortunately, six months after their arrival on the island, the family was moved to Athens where they were interviewed by the UN Refugee Agency. One month later, in October 2016, their application for resettlement was accepted by the Irish government.

'My mum had chosen about six countries. Where did I want to go in my mind? Maybe Holland or Sweden. Anywhere really, it didn't matter. I didn't know anything about Ireland, all I knew was they spoke English which was great for all of us. When I got the call from the Irish embassy I was flying in the sky. I was extremely happy. I met some Irish volunteers on Lesvos and they started telling me about their country. The only bad thing they mentioned was the weather. We were the lucky ones coming to Ireland. I was excited for a new life, everything would be starting from zero.'

In December 2016 the family arrived into Dublin airport with more than one hundred other Syrian refugees and were brought to the Mosney direct provision centre in Co Meath. They were told their refugee status and papers would be completed within three months and that they would be settled into houses by the spring. However, nearly a year later the family are still living in the direct provision centre.

'They told us that within three months our papers would be ready. But we ended up waiting month after month. We got our papers at the end of Ramadan which was in July. The way we are living in Mosney is not comfortable at all. They said it would be temporary but it's been ten months now with four people in a two-bedroom home. My mother is finally in a safe place but it's not the proper place for her. She's a teacher and wants to go out and teach. Many people in Dublin have asked her to come and teach Arabic but it's hard for her to travel there and back alone.' Maisa's younger sister was enrolled in a secondary school in Drogheda and is now in fifth year. Maisa kept busy by signing up for a course in interpretation and taking English lessons to improve her grammar. She began travelling to Dublin where she met Syrians who had already settled in Ireland and were able to offer guidance and support for new arrivals.

Before leaving Greece, Maisa had planned to jump straight back into her studies and apply for university as soon as she reached Ireland. However, she was told upon arrival that she would have to spend three years in the country before entering third level education. The only other option was to pay the expensive annual fees for international students. Instead of dwelling on this barrier to education, Maisa began investigating employment opportunities once the family had settled in Mosney. However, finding work as a Syrian refugee was not as easy as she had hoped. 'I was so tense sitting and doing nothing so I began asking around, but finding jobs in Ireland was difficult because the experience I had from home was different. I had to learn step by step and find a way to get back into education and finally enter university. It was either finding a way into education or finding a proper job that I could stick to, gain experience and have a living.'

In the summer of 2017, Maisa was introduced to an Irish man who had helped secure university scholarships for some other Syrian refugees. He offered to help the now twenty-year-old find the funding to continue her studies. 'I was not sure if my (secondary school) certificate would be accepted here because it was from a Syrian school in Turkey. I worried I would be facing the same issues I had in Turkey, that it would continue over here.' In August, Maisa was offered a place on the UCD pathway programme for students from abroad. The foundation course lasts one year and focuses on business, economics and social sciences. After completing the three-term programme, Maisa will be able to apply for a scholarship to study for a degree at UCD's Quinn School of Business.

'After getting this educational opportunity to study I finally feel young again. I'm back to being an actual twenty-year-old girl. Searching for a job and not being able to continue my education had made me feel old. I felt like I was growing up too fast. Everything still feels upside-down. I feel like my life will never be settled like the way it was before the war. I've grown up so much in the past two years and seen a lot in that time.'

Most of the Syrian families who arrived in Dublin with the Al-Hariri family in December 2016 have left Mosney and are living in houses in towns and cities across Ireland. Maisa is hopeful that her family will come next on the housing list and has requested to be settled close to Dublin so she can commute to and from UCD. 'It's been really hard not knowing if I can make any plans. It still makes me feel afraid at this point. But I have to carry on, even if I don't see anything coming from the government.' Shortly after their refugee status arrived, the Al-Hariri family applied for the youngest member of their family to join them in Ireland. Maisa's sister Amira was just thirteen the last time she saw her mother and sisters on that afternoon in March 2016. Their application for family reunification has been accepted and they are now working through the legalities to ensure Amira can travel to Ireland as soon as possible.

'She's turning sixteen in December which means she'll be able to make her own decision about coming to Ireland and living with her mother. We still don't know how long it will take for that to happen but thank God they accepted our family reunification application. It's been nearly two years since we last saw her.' Maisa knows that her father and brother will probably stay in Turkey but longs for the day when her whole family can be together again. 'It would mean everything to me. There's a real warmth between the members of my family and we feel that as long as we're together, we don't need anyone else. We can make it anywhere in the world if we're together.'

2017 Migration

In January 2017 the historian Timothy Garton Ash wrote that had he been cryogenically frozen in January 2005, he would have gone to his 'provisional rest as a happy European'. However, were he to wake up from this deep freeze 12 years later, he would have immediately died from shock: 'For now there is crisis and disintegration wherever I look. The Eurozone is chronically dysfunctional, sunlit Athens is plunged into misery, young Spaniards with doctorates are reduced to serving as waiters in London or Berlin, the children of Portuguese friends seek work in Brazil and Angola, and the periphery of Europe is diverging from its core ... The glorious freedom of movement for young Poles and other Central and Eastern Europeans has now contributed substantially to a shocking referendum vote by my own country, Britain, to leave the EU altogether. And Brexit brings with it the prospect of being stripped of my European citizenship on the thirtieth anniversary of 1989.'[60]

Garton Ash was not the only European commentator to proclaim in 2017 an inherently pessimistic outlook for the future of the EU and western democracy as we know it. Ivan Krastov wrote that Brexit and the election of Donald Trump had 'upended future predictions of Europe's survival'. 'Major terrorists attacks in a European capital, or armed conflict and a new wave of refugees on Europe's periphery, could easily bring the union to the edge of collapse. Democracy in Europe, which had long been an instrument for inclusion, is now slowly being transformed into a tool for exclusion. The dream (now fantasy) of a Europe without frontiers is being replaced by the grim reality of a barricaded continent.'[61]

On 20 January Donald Trump was sworn in as the president of the United States. What followed was a year of impulsive behaviour; hateful rhetoric, often through the medium of early morning tweets; chaotic White House management and battles to reverse or undermine numerous policies implemented by his predecessor. Shortly after his inauguration, Trump signed an executive order temporarily halting travel from six majority-Muslim countries. He rejected claims that the move was a 'Muslim ban', accusing the media of spreading 'fake news', and argued that America remained 'a proud nation of immigrants' that would 'continue to show compassion to those fleeing oppression, but we will do so while protecting our own citizens and borders'. The order barred people from Syria, Iran, Libya, Somalia, Chad and Yemen from entering the US and also introduced a cap of 50,000 refugees to be accepted in 2017, down from the 110,000 set by Barack Obama. The ban came into full effect in December 2017.

In September immigrants in the United States took another hit when Trump announced he was ending the Daca—Deferred Action for Childhood Arrivals—programme which gave work permits to people who had come to the US illegally as children. The federal programme, created in 2012 under Barack Obama, protected nearly 800,000 young adult immigrants from deportation and allowed them to work legally.

In June Trump announced he was pulling the United States out of the Paris Climate Change accord—the legally binding climate deal adopted by 195 countries in December 2015. Trump argued that the agreement would hurt the US economy and gave other countries an unfair advantage. His absence was notable from the One World Summit in Paris in December 2017 which brought together heads of state with US billionaires and film stars to discuss the latest efforts to tackle global warming. California governor Jerry Brown told the event that the fires which had ravaged his state through the year were just a hint of the 'lethal waves' to come. 'The migration problems in Europe are nothing to what they will be when the Mediterranean burns up,' he said.

In May France brought a temporary halt to the rise to power of the far-right across some EU nations, when thirty-nine-year-old pro-European Emmanuel Macron was elected president, defeating Front National leader Marine Le Pen. The UK's general election saw Britain's young people leading a surge in support for Jeremy Corbyn's Labour Party, leaving Theresa May's Conservatives barely hanging onto power through a deal with Northern Ireland's DUP. In Germany the September elections led to months of inconclusive inter-party negotiations after Angela Merkel and her centre-right Christian Democratic Union party's share of the vote collapsed; a collapse largely attributed to her generous but unpopular refugee policy in 2015. The biggest winner was the anti-immigration Alternative for Germany (AfD) party which came from nowhere to become the third-largest party with nearly 13% of the vote.

2017 was not immune to the spate of terrorist attacks that had occurred across Europe in previous years. The UK experienced a number of violent attacks, the most serious of which resulted in the deaths of 22 people, including children, after a suicide bomber detonated a homemade bomb at the entrance to the Manchester Arena in May where thousands of teenage and young adult fans had gathered to hear pop singer Ariana Grande. In August a van drove onto the crowded Las Ramblas boulevard in Barcelona killing 14 people, while another person was killed in the same way in nearby Cambrils.

Speaking at the UN in September Donald Tusk, President of the European Council, called for a strengthening of the global fight against terrorism and violent extremism. 'In short,' he said, 'we must be more determined than they are.' Two months later, UN secretary general António Guterres said the only way to prevent 'a vicious circle of instability and resentment' was through upholding human rights and the rule of law. He reiterated that despite the rise of attacks in Europe, most terrorism continued to take place in developing countries, with three-quarters of all terrorism-related deaths occurring in Iraq, Afghanistan, Syria, Nigeria and Somalia.

'Terrorism thrives wherever there is resentment, humiliation, lack of education,' he said. 'Terrorism thrives when disenfranchised people meet nothing but indifference and nihilism. It is deeply rooted in hopelessness and despair. That is why human rights, all human rights, including economic, social and cultural rights, are unquestionably a part of the solution in fighting terrorism.' Mr Guterres also criticised the media for focusing too much on attacks carried out by immigrants and blaming specific communities for extremist acts. 'Refugees fleeing conflict are frequently targeted. It is a horrible distortion of their plight, to accuse victims of terrorism of the crime they have just fled.'

In the midst of a housing crisis, Ireland's Department of Justice admitted that it was struggling to house the small number of Syrian refugees arriving from Greece and Lebanon and that it had considered suspending the resettlement and relocation programme due to capacity issues in accommodation. By December some 1,400 people, predominantly Syrians, had arrived in Ireland under the Irish Refugee Protection Programme. While the number of refugee arrivals under the programme did increase throughout the year, the government continued to fall far short of its original commitment of taking in 4,000 people by the end of 2017. No asylum seekers arrived from Italy, with the Department blaming the 'refusal of Italy to allow security screenings' for the delay.

In November, after serious pressure from refugee support groups, the Irish Government introduced a new family reunification programme for refugees which would allow up to 530 family members into the State. However, Oxfam Ireland called for a greater definition of which family members would be eligible for the new programme, warning that separating refugees from elderly parents, siblings and children aged over eighteen was having 'a devastating impact'.

Ireland's 2017 immigration debate also centred around the right to work of asylum seekers living in direct provision centres. In May a Burmese man who had spent eight years in direct provision before getting refugee status won his Supreme Court appeal over laws which had prevented him seeking work as an asylum seeker. The court agreed that the ban was 'in principle' unconstitutional but adjourned making formal orders for six months to allow the government to take action. Retired High Court judge Bryan McMahon, who chaired a very critical 2015 report into the direct provision system, warned that the ban on working was 'positively harmful after a couple of years. These people are hollowed out. They become deskilled, depressed, isolated and institutionalised.' The Cabinet agreed to lift the ban while the Department of Justice proposed that asylum seekers would be allowed to participate in certain areas of the workforce after spending nine months in the direct provision system in line with practice in other EU countries. At the time of writing, legislation had not yet been introduced to ensure asylum seekers' right to work.

The results of the 2016 census, released throughout 2017, revealed that Ireland had firmly established itself as a desired destination for immigrants seeking work and study opportunities, as well as a far smaller number of arrivals seeking asylum. A total of 535,475 non-Irish nationals were recorded as living in the country, out of a total population of 4,761,865. Poles remained the largest non-national group with 122,515 people recorded, followed by 103,113 UK nationals and 36,552 Lithuanians. Poland, the UK, Lithuania, Romania, Latvia, Brazil, Spain, Italy, France, Germany, India and the US (in that order) all had more than 10,000 residents in Ireland, while Galway was named the 'most multicultural' city with 18.6% of its residents recorded as non-Irish. The census results also revealed Ireland was becoming an increasingly multi-lingual country, with 612,018 residents speaking a language other than Irish or English at home. As senior CSO statistician Deirdre Cullen noted following the release of the 2016 census migration and diversity results; 'non-Irish nationals and those with dual nationality are now well established in Irish society and communities throughout the country'.

Eve and Maybelle Wallis, 2017

Eve Wallis cried when she heard the news bulletin on the morning of 24 June, 2016. Her wife Maybelle had stayed up all night to watch the results of UK referendum to leave the European Union. The couple had already discussed leaving Birmingham if Brexit was passed, and now it was a reality. 'I had a really bad feeling about it because I'd been out leafleting in our local town centre,' remembers Maybelle. 'I've always been very pro-European and thought I'd best do my bit and go out and talk to people. The amount of bitterness and hate that you got made me feel I didn't want to live in that place. About 60% of the population voted to leave in the part of Birmingham where I worked.'

'The most articulate of them said Europe was holding us back economically and we needed to make our own trade deals but quite a lot of dialogue was centred around immigration. Even when I said 'I'm an immigrant and I work as a consultant in the NHS', that didn't seem to impress. It was very xenophobic. The younger women were more pro-European and the worst culprits were middle-aged and older men with some older women. A lot of people wouldn't even take the leaflet or listen; they'd already made up their minds. No amount of reasoning would move them.'

'There were also all the lies that Boris Johnson and Nigel Farage were coming out with,' adds Eve. 'It was absolute rubbish and of course they've all backtracked on it now. But how many people were tricked into voting to leave? We had fallen into real right wing territory and it was almost getting racist. You had right wing parties and the National Front going around on marches and flashing the Union Jack. It was starting to look a little like Germany before Nazism in the late 20s and early 30s. It wasn't just in Birmingham, it was England.'

Maybelle, who worked as a consultant pediatrician with the NHS, was also worried about the future of the British health service. 'Public services were getting increasingly dysfunctional. My job was really stressful and Eve's job was threatened by cuts. We felt we didn't have too much to lose by leaving. We had discussed it not only in the context of Brexit, but also in the context of austerity and how it was affecting our jobs; whether we could retire early and move abroad with the aim of finding somewhere cheaper to live using the money from downsizing on the property. We'd already started to look but it wasn't meant to be now, it was two to three years in the future. Then the referendum suddenly meant things would be more difficult. We were worried about freedom of movement and getting permission to settle abroad. People were talking about traitors and there was nasty language being used. It felt less free.'

'If we just sat back and took it easy who knew what would happen?' asks Eve. 'We could have moved to another European country and they would say sorry, you're no longer European, go back to England.' Maybelle's twenty-four-year-old son from a previous marriage had finished university and the couple had paid off the mortgage on their home. It felt like the right time to move. However, Brexit wasn't the only reason behind the couple's decision to leave Birmingham. In fact, it was for much more personal reasons that Eve and Maybelle packed up their trailer and took the ferry across the Irish Sea in January 2017.

Maybelle met Steve in 2001 through an online dating forum and soon afterwards the couple got married. The child of an American father and Taiwanese mother, Maybelle grew up and studied in London before moving to Birmingham in the mid 90s. 'Whenever anybody asks me where I'm from the answer is multi-faceted. I've always thought of myself primarily as being European because I was born in Brussels and I've always been conscious in Britain that I wasn't from around there. I felt foreign in Britain. Being European felt more inclusive.'

Steve, who is from Birmingham and was also previously married, spent nearly twelve years working as a service engineer and later as a diving instructor in Plymouth before moving back north where he met Maybelle. The couple had been married for ten years when Steve decided to 'come out' to his wife. He had recently been diagnosed with gynecomastia— when a man's breast tissue begins to swell– which he describes as a blessing in disguise. 'I wasn't totally disappointed with the news to be honest with you. It felt like I'd run out of maleness. I had struggled with the feeling most of my life but kept it under wraps and in the closet. Cross-dressing had happened but it was fairly infrequent. I thought I could deal with it but of course eventually you can't and it comes out. I realised the time for secrets was over, that I had to be who I really was.'

Maybelle was stunned when her husband announced he had decided to become a woman and change his name to Eve. 'It was completely out of the blue and was quite scary really. I had a very mixed reaction. The first thing I said was "great, we can go shopping for clothes together in London" but the following morning I got really upset. I just thought this is the end of our lives and the way we've lived up until now is forever changed. Eve had this secret for such a long time that she hadn't been honest about. That was really hurtful. In a way it's like bereavement because you lose the guy you thought you were married to and think now I'm living with a new person. I'm also a worrier and thought oh god, we'll never be able to go caravanning or cycling again because of other people's reactions.' Maybelle considered separation but eventually decided to stand by her partner. 'When the person you married is in their hour of need you can't just leave them.'

Meanwhile, Eve felt a deep sense of guilt for hiding such a huge secret from her wife for so long. She was also petrified by how friends, family and the general public would react to the truth. 'The reason it was secret in the first place was other people. You have no idea how hard it is to keep a secret and be absolutely terrified that someone might find out. Let's face it; society demands that if you are born with a penis, you dress like a man. If you're born with a vagina, you dress like a girl. You're either A or B. But have you not seen effeminate men or butch women? Gender is a wide spectrum.'

Most of Eve's loved ones, including her mother, responded very well to news of her transition. She attended a support group in Birmingham and gradually began to dress as a woman in public. 'My mum was fine about it, she didn't react negatively at all. She just said 'you know what you're doing'. She was probably one of the only mothers to come along to the Outskirts support group.' Maybelle's son was surprisingly unperturbed by the news. 'I think he was at uni when I came out,' says Eve. 'He'd come to visit for a weekend and we told him. We asked "would you like to see Steve dressed as Eve" and he said alright. Upstairs I went and put on some tights, a brown suede mini-skirt, an animal print top, a fur coat and the wig. I walked downstairs and he looks at me and says, "you look like Chewbacca". I was on the floor in bits laughing. He's so laid back.'

'It wasn't as bad as I thought it was going to be,' adds Maybelle. 'We could still go on holidays together and travel. It was also about letting our friends know what was going on and discovering that they still remained our friends and the world wasn't over. It was fun as well. You meet interesting people when you go to the gay quarter. They're all people who have had a bit of struggle for existence in a way and they've learned to look at situations from different perspectives. They're open-minded and you feel very safe around them.' The couple was very surprised to discover that a close friend was also transgender and like Eve, had been hiding the truth for years. 'What really helped us was that couple who we had known for years,' says Maybelle. 'The husband is also trans although he is much more 'closet' about it. But it helped to normalise it. We felt like we weren't the only people encountering this.'

Eve's GP was supportive of her decision and prescribed oestrogen patches. She later travelled to London for an appointment with an endocrinologist where she discovered she already had a very low testosterone count. 'The doctor took me off the patches, put me on tablets and I had to have testosterone blocking injections every twelve weeks. It brought home that feeling that I had run out of maleness. Before then I'd always been very over the top with my interests. I was a biker, a diver, a maintenance fitter; all very male things. Perhaps it was to counter the female side.'

Her boss and colleagues at Worcester County Council also responded well when she told them about her decision to change her name and live as a woman. 'I told some of the immediate team, the health and safety team, one by one over a period of two to three months and they responded magnificently. I also had a meeting with my manager, the corporate health and safety manager and the head of HR. She put things into action straight away and said we'll send an email out to everyone explaining straight off that Eve is female now and will be using the female toilets. It was very matter of fact and they wished me well. I never had any problems.' In some ways, Eve found that being a female health and safety manager actually made her job easier. 'I guess beforehand they thought I was a bit hard-faced and dogmatic but then they saw a softer side and they responded well to it. Being female made me more approachable.'

Unfortunately, the couple's neighbours in their home town of Bromsgrove on the outskirts of Birmingham were not as comfortable with the news. 'Living in the suburbs of Birmingham we had never really made friends among our neighbours, even before Eve's transition,' says Maybelle. 'Her appearances "en femme" were met with some cold stares from across the street. One woman would point Eve out to her friend if she saw her driving past.'

After the results of the Brexit referendum the couple began organising the move to Ireland. They admit they were nervous about living in a country which up until very recently had been known for its conservative and religious views. 'We were apprehensive about relocating to Ireland and feared we might not be accepted but at the same time we felt we had nothing to lose,' says Maybelle. 'Having been uncomfortable in our own back yard we wanted to try and live somewhere where we felt there was going to be some acceptance. Ireland sort of fitted the bill in that it was European and English speaking so I could get a job. It was a place where we could live in a rural environment and I could still be close to work. With Ireland there had always been a sort of special arrangement anyway driven by Northern Ireland and the Border. It seemed unlikely our rights would be curtailed here because those arrangements pre-date the European Union.'

Maybelle applied for work in hospitals across Ireland through a recruitment agency in Dublin who also put the couple in touch with TENI (Transgender Equality Network Ireland). They travelled around the country while Maybelle interviewed for different positions and eventually settled on Wexford where they bought a house. 'By the time of my interview in Wexford, Eve and I had traversed much of Ireland taking in Galway, Tralee, Ballinasloe, Letterkenny and Dublin. We were struck by the courtesy and friendliness of the people we met and by being able to walk around the towns without getting disapproving glances. In Dublin we were surprised by the way in which it's normal for groups of women of various ages to be out for a drink in the pub, whilst in Birmingham women are often made to feel that the pub is still mostly a male preserve. While there may be some way to go in terms of feminist legislation—the law on abortion, for example—I do feel this greater sense of freedom and equality here that makes it easier for people to be transgender.'

Eve was particularly grateful to the older Irish women who called her 'love' and 'dear' in small rural shops and cafes. 'It's excellent to be treated the way that I feel. It gives me a glow inside because it's what I want to be. I've never made any secret of the fact that I'm transgender, I'm not trying to fool anybody. I'm not doing this to fool blokes into having sex with me. Sex has got nothing to do with it. It's gender, not sex. I haven't changed sexual preference-wise. I am who I am.'

In April 2017, Eve travelled to India for gender reassignment surgery. She had spent months researching clinics and settled on New Delhi after meeting two English women who had already undergone the procedure in India. 'I was on an NHS list but you have to wait eighteen months for the surgery in the UK and that was miles away. To do it privately would have cost in excess of £20,000 (€22,600). I paid $7,300 (€6,250) in India.' Eve returned to Ireland in mid-May after more than four weeks in India and spent a couple of months at home relaxing. Asked if she's happy with the results she says 'yes' without a moment's hesitation. 'Would I go back to being a man? That's the million dollar question. But no, I wouldn't.'

Despite their initial reservations about the move to Ireland, the couple says Wexford now feels like home. 'Within four days of picking up the keys we were in a nearby bar making friends and on the following evening about twelve people came to our housewarming,' says Maybelle. 'They accept Eve as she is, whether she's doing DIY jobs in her scruffs, or made up and tidy for a night out.' Eve has only had one negative experience since the move when she contacted a lingerie shop to arrange a bra fitting. 'I explained to her I'd just had my implants done and she said you can't use the changing rooms, they're only for women. I said "excuse me, I'm fully transgendered" and she said, "yes, I know." So I put the phone down.' Eve prefers when people ask outright what it feels like to be transgender rather than make assumptions behind her back. 'It gets the message out and I can give a quick history about my experience. I say I've never been gay and never had anal sex and so you can dispel that myth straight off. If anything I'm probably a lesbian now.'

Eve says Irish society is far more accepting of the transgender people than most European countries. However, the process of actually transitioning in Ireland is far more complicated than abroad due to a lack of services. 'It's not a lack of skill, I think Irish doctors are as good as English doctors, in some cases better,' says Eve. 'But it's in terms of access to treatment. Why isn't there transgender surgery being carried out in this country and why are people being sent to the UK? There's such a limited number of endocrinologists who will treat trans people under the HSE. Let's say I decided here in Ireland that I was trans and I need hormones. Where do I get those hormones? The GP can't prescribe them unless he's got authorisation from a specialist.'

'I get the feeling that it's still quite difficult for young people here to embark on that transition process,' adds Maybelle. 'We've arrived in Ireland with Eve almost fully transgender but starting that process seems to be an issue here.'

Maybelle is very happy with her work as a paediatrician at Wexford General Hospital. 'In the hospital corridors, I've learned to walk more slowly than in the UK; we don't barrel along avoiding eye contact and it is the correct etiquette to take a little time to greet others and exchange pleasantries. At the same time, the morning ward round proceeds at a brisk rate. In my previous job, getting a nurse to stay with me for the round and focus on the patients without rushing off to do something else was near impossible. It's not about having an entourage—it's about working together on the patient's treatment plan and communicating clearly with the families.'

'There are problems here like long waiting lists for outpatient appointments and investigations and an over-reliance on Dublin for specialist treatment, but there is not the dysfunctionality of today's NHS. I think the Irish people tend to perceive their health service as being rubbish and that the NHS is brilliant. But there are aspects where the HSE is better than the UK at the moment and they're probably not aware of that.'

The couple is now focusing on refurbishing their new home and Eve hopes to find part-time work and get involved with volunteering in the local area. 'Socially here it's a real little community and people have accepted us very warmly,' says Maybelle. 'Birmingham is a fading memory. Now we have a house high on a hill among golden gorse and pine trees. At the back of the house we have a distant view of Rosslare and on a clear day, it is possible to see Wales as a tiny grey streak on the horizon.'

Endnotes

1. 'European history in the making'. *The Irish Times*, 1 May 2004.
2. O'Brennan, John. 'The success of the eastern EU enlargement debunks current fears'. *The Guardian*, 19 January 2013.
3. Ní Mhurchú, Aoileann. 'Rethinking citizenship: revisiting the 2004 Irish Citizenship Referendum a decade later'. Open Democracy, 7 August 2014, https://www.opendemocracy.net/can-europe-make-it/aoileann-n%C3%AD-mhurch%C3%BA/rethinking-citizenship-revisiting-2004-irish-citizenship-refe.
4. Staunton, Denis. 'Leaders attend historic flag-raising ceremony at Aras an Uachtarain', *The Irish Times*, 3 May 2004.
5. Garton Ash, Timothy. 'Is Europe Disintegrating?', *The New York Review of Books*, 19 January 2017.
6. European Union, Technical Mission to Morocco. *Visit to Ceuta and Melilla – Mission Report Technical mission to Morocco on illegal immigration 7th October–11th October 2005*, 18 October 2005.
7. *Ibid.*
8. 'Statement by the Minister regarding the Real Facts about the Asylum and Deportation Systems', Irish Naturalisation and Immigration Service, 7 June 2005, http://www.inis.gov.ie/en/INIS/Pages/PR07000171.
9. *Ibid.*
10. Ahern, Bertie. 'Foreword to Planning For Diversity The National Action Plan Against Racism 2005-2008', Department of Justice, Equality and Law Reform, 2005, http://www.justice.ie/en/JELR/NPARen.pdf/Files/NPARen.pdf.
11. Ricklef Beutin, Marcel Canoy, Anna Horvath, Agnes Hubert, Frédéric Lerais, Peter Smith and Myriam Sochacki. European Commission, Bureau of European Policy Advisors. *Migration and public perception*, 4 October 2006.
12. Cartner, Holly. 'EU: Outsourcing Migration Control Puts Human Rights at Risk', Human Rights Watch, 15 October 2006, https://www.

hrw.org/news/2006/10/15/eu-outsourcing-migration-control-puts-human-rights-risk.

13. Mooten, Nalinie. 'Making Separated Children Visible', The Irish Refugee Council, 2006, https://www.pobal.ie/Publications/Documents/Making%20Separated%20Children%20Visible%20-%20Irish%20Refugee%20Council%20-%202006.pdf.

14. Rosenstock-Armie, Héilean. 'All children in Ireland should be cherished equally', The Irish Times, 23 June 2006.

15. 'Missing asylum seeker children "failed by State"', The Irish Times, 2 August 2006.

16. 'Plea over temporary residency for trafficking victims', The Irish Times, 28 August 2006.

17. O'Donoghue, Siobhan. Foreword to Realising Integration: Creating the Conditions for the Economic, Social, Political and Cultural Inclusion Of Migrant Workers and their Families in Ireland, Migrant Rights Centre Ireland, July 2006.

18. Ibid.

19. Mac Cormaic, Ruadhán. 'No man's land where you cannot work and must live on €19 a week', The Irish Times, 6 June 2007.

20. Loyal, Steven. 'Getting our heads around reality of multiculturalism', The Irish Times, 22 August 2007.

21. 'Iraq: Neighbors Stem Flow of Iraqis Fleeing War: US and UK Bear Special Duty to Aid Refugees', Human Rights Watch, 16 April 2007, https://www.hrw.org/news/2007/04/16/iraq-neighbors-stem-flow-iraqis-fleeing-war.

22. Sciolino, Elaine. 'Immigration, Black Sheep and Swiss Rage', New York Times, 8 October 2007.

23. Migration Nation: Statement on Integration Strategy and Diversity Management, Office of the Minister for Integration, 1 May 2008, http://www.integration.ie/website/omi/omiwebv6.nsf/page/AXBN-7SQDF91044205-en/$File/Migration%20Nation.pdf.

24. O'Brien, Dan. 'Origins of the Great Recession', The Irish Times, 12 September 2013.

25. Barrett, Alan and Elish Kelly. 'The Impact of Ireland's Recession on the Labour Market Outcomes of its Immigrants', ESRI Working Paper No. 355, ESRI, September 2010.

26. Legrain, Philippe. 'Tear Down the Walls', The Guardian, 8 August 2008.

27. Lacy Swing, William. Foreword to Migration, Environment and Climate Change: Assessing the Evidence (eds. Frank Laczko and Christine Aghazarm), International Organization for Migration, 2009.

28. 'PM to "tighten" migration rules', BBC News, 12 November 2009.

29. Allen, Peter. 'French police detain hundreds of migrants in raid on Calais "jungle"', The Telegraph, 22 September 2009.

30. Audi, Nadim and Caroline Brothers. 'French Police Dismantle Migrant Camp', *The New York Times*, 22 September 2009.
31. Henry, Lesley-Anne and Lisa Smyth. 'Shameful scenes as Romanians flee homes', *Belfast Telegraph*, 18 June 2009.
32. McKittrick, David. 'Belfast mob "threatened to kill Romanian children"', *Independent*, 17 June 2009.
33. Meredith, Fionola. 'Bigotry in Belfast', *The Guardian*, 17 June 2009.
34. Reilly, Catherine. 'What generation hostel did next', *The Irish Times*, 7 May 2010.
35. 'Separated Children in Foster Care Seminar Paper', Barnardos, 28 September 2011.
36. 'Submission to the UN CERD Committee on the Examination of Ireland's Combined Third and Fourth Periodic Reports', Irish Human Rights Commission, November 2010, https://www.ihrec.ie/download/pdf/20101210101458.pdf.
37. Krastev, Ivan. *After Europe* (Philadelphia: University of Pennsylvania Press, 2017).
38. Price, John. 'What did the Arab Spring Achieve?', International Policy Digest, 30 July 2014, https://intpolicydigest.org/2014/07/30/what-did-the-arab-spring-achieve/.
39. 'Top 10 of 2011 - Issue #1: Arab Spring and Fear of Migrant Surge Expose Rift in EU Immigration Policy Circles', Migration Policy Institute, 1 December 2011, https://www.migrationpolicy.org/article/top-10-2011-issue-1-arab-spring-and-fear-migrant-surge-expose-rift-eu-immigration-policy.
40. 'Strategy Statement 2011-2014', Department of Justice and Equality, 2011, http://www.justice.ie/en/JELR/Strategy%20Statement%20_English_%202011-2014.pdf/Files/Strategy%20Statement%20_English_%202011-2014.pdf.
41. Cooper, Rob. 'Rise of the Greek neo-Nazis: Ultra-right party Golden Dawn wants to force immigrants into work camps and plant landmines along Turkish border', *Daily Mail*, 7 May 2012.
42. McGinnity, Frances, Emma Quinn, Gillian Kingston and Philip O'Connell. 'Annual Monitoring Report on Integration 2013', Economic and Social Research Institute and The Integration Centre, June 2014, https://www.esri.ie/pubs/BKMNEXT266.pdf.
43. Power, Jim Power and Péter Szlovak. *Migrants and the Irish Economy*. The Integration Centre, 2012.
44. Kirby, Emma Jane. *The Optician of Lampedusa* (London: Allen Lane, 2016).
45. Shenker, Jack. 'Mediterranean migrant deaths: a litany of largely avoidable loss', *The Guardian*, 3 October 2013.
46. 'Lampedusa follow up: concrete actions to prevent loss of life in the Mediterranean and better address migratory and asylum flows',

European Commission Press Release, 4 December 2013, http://europa.eu/rapid/press-release_IP-13-1199_en.htm.

47. Obama, Barack. 'President Obama's Sept. 10 speech on Syria'. *The Washington Post*, 10 September 2013.

48. 'UN Inquiry reports gross human rights violations in Eritrea', United Nations Human Rights Office of the High Commissioner, 8 June 2015, http://www.ohchr.org/en/NewsEvents/Pages/DisplayNews.aspx?NewsID=16054.

49. Obama, Barack. 'President Obama's Speech on Combating ISIS and Terrorism', CNN Politics, 11 September 2014.

50. O'Brian, Carl and Sinead O'Shea. 'Could direct provision be the subject of a future government apology?', *The Irish Times*, 12 August 2014.

51. Gunter, Joel. 'Alan Kurdi: Why one picture cut through', BBC News, 4 September 2015.

52. *Ibid.*

53. 'It is time to end this migrant madness', *Daily Mail* Comment, 30 July 2015.

54. Jones, Sam. 'Paris attacks: France's year of terror', *Financial Times*, 15 November 2015.

55. Mac Cormaic, Ruadhán. 'Power to the people: Year of the populist revolt', *The Irish Times*, 29 December 2016.

56. Krastev, Ivan. *After Europe* (Philadelphia: University of Pennsylvania Press, 2017).

57. 'Statement on the refugee crisis and the EU-Turkey agreement', Irish Human Rights and Equality Commission, 8 April 2016, https://www.ihrec.ie/statement-on-the-refugee-crisis-and-the-eu-turkey-agreement/.

58. 'Hitting Rock Bottom: How 2016 Became the Worst Year For Syria's Children', Unicef, 13 March 2017, https://www.unicef.org/media/media_95077.html.

59. Dearden, Lizzie. 'UN report finds no evidence migration causes terror attacks and warns anti-refugee laws could worsen risk', *Independent*, 24 October 2016.

60. Garton Ash, Timothy. 'Is Europe Disintegrating?', *The New York Review of Books*, 19 January 2017.

61. Krastev, Ivan. *After Europe* (Philadelphia: University of Pennsylvania Press, 2017).

Author's Note

New to the Parish began as a temporary three-month series in *The Irish Times*. I was asked to provide up to ten articles to help fill the newspaper during the quiet summer months of 2015. I lined up the first interview with the partner of a friend. I knew her boyfriend had an unusual story and hoped his experience might interest readers. The second interview was with a woman I met at a party, the third through a contact at work. Meanwhile, I sent out dozens of emails to community groups, refugee organisations, policy makers and student clubs in the hope that a handful of people would respond and be willing to talk about their journey to Ireland. Bit by bit, messages began to appear in my inbox: a man from Pakistan, a woman from California, a family from Syria, a couple from Argentina. But one fear persisted throughout that summer; what would happen when the stories ran out? How many people would actually be willing to share the intimate details of their lives with an Irish journalist? I need never have worried. It quickly became apparent that no matter how shy or reserved a person was when we first met, every single one of them had something to say. Almost three years later, these voices continue to speak out through the weekly New to the Parish article in the pages of *The Irish Times*.

There may be more than seven billion of us on earth, but as Ernest Hemingway so aptly put it, 'any man's life, told truly, is a novel'. That was the goal of the New to the Parish series and in turn became the goal of this book: to show readers that regardless of background, upbringing, class or religion, every person has a story. I also aimed to show how Ireland has radically changed over recent decades, transforming from a country of large-scale emigration into an increasingly diverse nation of immigrants. Ireland has moved far from its former status as one of Western Europe's poorest countries to become a globalised nation of opportunities. Our small republic of 4.7 million people has many flaws and we do not boast a proud history of open-door policies to outsiders. However, we have, in recent years, succeeded in largely avoiding the extreme-right, xenophobic political presence that has begun to raise its ugly head in so many other European nations. Many claim that the Irish people's historical hindsight of being rejected in foreign lands has played an important role in our willingness to welcome outsiders. While I sometimes struggle to believe that our mass exodus abroad in the nineteenth and twentieth centuries has made us more compassionate towards immigrants than other European nations, I do hope we can draw on this recent history to develop a strong national consciousness and acceptance of the women, men and children who have chosen to come to Ireland to build a better life.

Working on New to the Parish has taught me that truly telling a person's story means more than just asking questions; it requires empathy and understanding. The fourteen people, couples and families I interviewed for this book entrusted me with the stories of their lives. In return, I hope I have recounted their tales in a respectful, honest and insightful way. Let me reiterate that this book is not a history of migration to Ireland, nor is it a detailed analysis of the numerous migration crises that have taken place around the world in recent years. It is my attempt, as an Irish journalist with a deep interest in human migration, to give readers a better understanding of what it means to be a migrant in the twenty-first century. I hope that these stories will inspire and encourage people to move away from the anti-immigrant, sometimes hate-filled, often fractious rhetoric which filters into our daily newsfeeds. New to the Parish is a reminder that every migrant is a human being; a person who loves, fears, dreams, hopes and strives for happiness.

Acknowledgements

To Bassam, Magda, George, Azeez, Tibor, Aniko, David, Akos, Rafique, Rafika, Jamalida, Waheeda, Zeenie, Carlinhos, Sorcha, Chandrika, Mabel, Flavia, Ellen, James, Maisa, Eve and Maybelle. Without your stories New to the Parish would not have been possible. Your willingness to speak about your lives is the reason I was able to write this book and I am honoured that you chose to share these experiences with me.

To every single person that has featured in *The Irish Times* New to the Parish series I must also thank you. From the very first article in July 2015 you have given readers across Ireland the chance to learn about the latest arrivals to Irish shores and develop an understanding of how it feels to start over. It can't have been easy to speak so openly of the challenges and hardships many of you have encountered but your stories are so important, now more than ever.

Thank you to all the organisations who have helped me contact different communities across Ireland and introduced me to so many interviewees. Thank you to New Island Books, especially Dan Bolger and Stephen Reid, for expressing an interest in New to the Parish and publishing this book. Thank you to Clare Henderson, Erin McClure and Kate Hynes for

229

the artistic advice on cover ideas. Thank you to Kate Gaughran for the final design for this book.

Thank you to Roisín Ingle for coming to me with the idea for this series nearly three years ago and for the unwavering support through every article. Thank you to Kevin O'Sullivan for believing in the series in its early days and to Paul O'Neill and Deirdre Veldon for supporting this book. Also at *The Irish Times*, thank you to Mark Hennessy, Ruadhán Mac Cormaic, Carl O'Brien, Kathy Sheridan, Rosita Boland, Malachy Clerkin, Conor Goodman and David Labanyi for the journalistic advice, guidance and encouragement these past few years.

Thank you to the talented photographers who gave their time to the series and produced such beautiful portraits for this book: Dara Mac Dónaill, Brenda Fitzsimons, Alan Betson, Cyril Byrne, Nick Bradshaw, Dave Meehan, Patrick Byrne, James Connolly and Sarah Freund. Also thanks to *The Irish Times* video team—Kathleen Harris, Bryan O'Brien and Enda O'Dowd—for the powerful video pieces you filmed and produced during the series.

Thank you to all my friends and family for the endless support in the final few months of writing. A special thanks to Maeve O'Rourke, Ciarán Murphy and Gillian Todd for reading over chapters at short notice. To my sister Gráinne, thank you for being a rock during those moments of self-doubt and apprehension. To my parents Doireann and Andy, thank you for giving me the opportunities that have brought me this far, for acting as editorial consultants during this entire writing process and for your love. And finally to Mark Horgan, for the love and inspiration and for believing in me every step of the way.